modern religious poems

modern

religious

poems

A CONTEMPORARY ANTHOLOGY

EDITED BY JACOB TRAPP

HARPER & ROW, PUBLISHERS

NEW YORK, EVANSTON, AND LONDON

FIRST EDITION

Library of Congress Catalog Card Number: 64-14371

D-O

acknowledgments

Grateful acknowledgment is made to the following publishers and individuals for permission to reprint selections from the works indicated:

GEORGE ALLEN & UNWIN, LTD., London, for "A Christmas Carol" from *Selected Poems* by Gilbert Thomas.

BURNS & OATES, LTD., London, for "Advent Meditation," "Unto Us a Son is Given," and "The Newer Vainglory" from *Poems* by Alice Meynell.

JONATHAN CAPE, LTD., London, for "A Greeting," "Mangers," "Speed," and "Cant" from *Collected Poems* by W. H. Davies.

COWARD-MCCANN, New York, for "Bread the Holy" from *Compass Rose* by Elizabeth J. Coatsworth (copyright 1929 by Coward-Mc-Cann).

JOHN DAY COMPANY, INC., Publishers, New York, for "Light" and "Noah" from *Combat at Midnight* by Herman Hagedorn (copyright 1940 by Herman Hagedorn).

DODD, MEAD & COMPANY, New York, for "The House of Christmas" and "The Sword of Surprise" from *The Collected Poems* by G. K. Chesterton (copyright 1932 by Dodd, Mead & Company, Inc.).

DOUBLEDAY & COMPANY, INC., New York, for "At a Solemn Musick" (copyright 1958 by Delmore Schwartz) and "Holderlin" (copyright 1954 by Delmore Schwartz) from *Summer Knowledge* by Delmore Schwartz; "Jacob and the Angel" (copyright 1959 by Brother Antoninus) from *The Hazards of Holiness* by Brother Antoninus; "Testament," "For Simone Weil," "The Contemplative," and "Interrogative" from *Moment in Ostia* by Sister M. Therése (copyright 1959 by Doubleday & Company, Inc.).

E. P. DUTTON & COMPANY, INC., New York, for "In This Strange House," "Invocation," and "A Small Thought Speaks for the Flesh" from *Cloud above Clocktime* by Carleton Drewry (copyright 1957 by Carleton Drewry); "A Song in Humility" from *A Time of Turning* by Carleton Drewry (copyright 1951 by E. P. Dutton & Company, Inc.); "I Said to the Leaf" from *The Sounding Summer* by Carleton Drewry (copyright 1948 by E. P. Dutton & Company, Inc.).

NORMA MILLAY ELLIS for "God's World" and "Dirge without Music" from *Collected Poems* by Edna St. Vincent Millay, published by Harper & Brothers (copyright 1913, 1928, 1940, 1955 by Edna St. Vincent Millay and Norma Millay Ellis).

FABER & FABER, LTD., London, for "The Church" from *Collected Poems 1921–1958* by Edwin Muir.

FARRAR, STRAUS & COMPANY, INC., for "Crucifix" and "Essay on Deity" from *The Scarecrow Christ* by Elder Olson (copyright 1954 by Elder Olson).

GROVE PRESS, INC., New York, for "Abraham," "The Good Man in Hell," "The Absent," and "The Killing" from *Collected Poems 1921–1951* by Edwin Muir (copyright 1957 by Edwin Muir).

HARCOURT, BRACE & WORLD, New York, for "i thank You God" from *Poems 1923–1954* by e e cummings (copyright 1950 by e e cummings); "may my heart be always open" from *Poems 1923–1954* by e e cummings (copyright 1938 by e e cummings); "i am a little church (no great cathedral)" from *95 Poems* by e e cummings (copyright 1958 by

5

e e cummings; "The Fundament is Shifted" from *Fact of Crystal* by Abbie Huston Evans (first published in *The New Yorker*, copyright 1961 by Abbie Huston Evans); "Journey of the Magi" from *Collected Poems* by T. S. Eliot (copyright 1936 by Harcourt, Brace & World, 1963 by T. S. Eliot); "O Light Invisible" and "Why Should Men Love the Church?" from *The Rock* by T. S. Eliot (copyright Harcourt, Brace & World, 1934, T. S. Eliot, 1962); "A Christmas Hymn" from *Advice to a Prophet and Other Poems* by Richard Wilbur (copyright 1961 by Richard Wilbur); "Advice to a Prophet" from *Advice to a Prophet and Other Poems* by Richard Wilbur (first published in *The New Yorker*, copyright 1959 by Richard Wilbur); "Prayer to go to Paradise with the Donkeys" from *Things of This World* by Richard Wilbur (translation from Francis Jammes, copyright 1956 by Richard Wilbur); "For You" from *Smoke and Steel* by Carl Sandburg (copyright 1920 by Harcourt, Brace & World, 1948 by Carl Sandburg); "Upstream" from *Slabs of the Sunburnt West* by Carl Sandburg (copyright 1922 by Harcourt, Brace & World, 1950 by Carl Sandburg); "Special Starlight" from *Complete Poems* by Carl Sandburg (copyright 1950 by Carl Sandburg); "Presence" and "Closing Cadence" from *The Living Seed* by John Moffit (copyright 1962 by John Moffit); "Jonah" from *The Seven League Crutches* by Randall Jarrell (copyright 1951 by Randall Jarrell).

HARPER & ROW, PUBLISHERS, INC., New York, for "Any Human to Another" from *On These I Stand* by Countee Cullen (copyright 1935 by Harper & Brothers, 1963 by Ida M. Cullen); "The Litany of the Dark People" from *On These I Stand* by Countee Cullen (copyright 1927 by Harper & Brothers, 1955 by Ida M. Cullen); "Even in the Darkness" from *Balm in Gilead* by Helene Mullins (copyright 1930 by Harper & Brothers, 1958 by Helene Mullins); "Our Father" from *Lord Juggler and Other Poems* by Roberta Teale Swartz (copyright 1932 by Harper & Brothers, 1960 by Roberta Teale Swartz); "Saint John" from *Atlas and Beyond* by Elizabeth J. Coatsworth (copyright 1924 by Harper & Brothers, 1952 by Elizabeth J. Coatsworth); selection from "The Eleventh Commandment" and "Prayer on the Night before Easter" from *The Fortune Teller* by John Holmes (copyright 1954 by John Holmes).

HARVARD UNIVERSITY PRESS for Poems 1459, 712, 792, 1078, and 1691 from *The Poems of Emily Dickinson* edited by Thomas H. Johnson (copyright 1951, 1955 by the President and Fellows of Harvard College).

HILL & WANG, INC., PUBLISHERS, New York, for "The God of Galaxies," "Never Another," "Praise Doubt," and "Let There Be Law" from *Collected Poems* by Mark Van Doren (copyright 1963 by Mark Van Doren).

HOLT, RINEHART & WINSTON, INC., New York, for "A Prayer in Spring," "The Peaceful Shepherd," "Acceptance," "I Could Give All to Time," and "The Fear of God" from *Complete Poems* by Robert Frost (copyright 1928, 1930, 1934, 1939, 1947 by Holt, Rinehart & Winston, Inc., 1942 by Robert Frost, renewed 1956, 1962 by Robert Frost); 33 lines from "A Masque of Reason," title of poem and book by Robert Frost (copyright 1945 by Holt, Rinehart & Winston, Inc.); "But God's Own Descent" from *In the Clearing* by Robert Frost (copyright

1956, 1962 by Robert Frost); "After Sunset" from *Wilderness Songs* by Grace Hazard Conkling (copyright 1920 by Holt, Rinehart & Winston, Inc., renewed 1948 by Grace Hazard Conkling).

LITTLE, BROWN & COMPANY, Boston, for "Benediction" from *Selected Poems 1928–1958* by Stanley Kunitz (copyright 1956 by Stanley Kunitz); "The Overtakelessness of Those" from *The Complete Poems of Emily Dickinson* (copyright 1914, 1942 by Martha Dickinson Bianchi).

THE MACMILLAN COMPANY, New York, for "And There Was a Great Calm," "God's Education," "In the Servants' Quarters," "In Time of 'The Breaking of Nations,'" "Let Me Enjoy," "The Oxen," and "Tolerance" from *Collected Poems* by Thomas Hardy (copyright 1925 by The Macmillan Company); "Unkept Good Fridays" from *Winter Words* by Thomas Hardy (copyright 1928 by Florence E. Hardy and Sydney E. Cockerell, 1956 by Lloyds Bank, Ltd.); "Easter Song" from *Windward Rock* by Kenneth Leslie (copyright 1934 by The Macmillan Company); from *Collected Poems* by Vachel Lindsay: "Johnny Appleseed's Hymn" (copyright 1925 by The Macmillan Company), "The Leaden-eyed" and "Abraham Lincoln Walks at Midnight" (copyright 1914 by The Macmillan Company, 1942 by Elizabeth C. Lindsay), "How Samson Bore Away the Gates of Gaza" (copyright 1917 by The Macmillan Company, 1945 by Elizabeth C. Lindsay), "On the Building of Springfield," "Incense," and "The Eagle that is Forgotten" (copyright 1913 by The Macmillan Company), stanzas from "Litany of the Heroes" (copyright 1923 by The Macmillan Company), "Springfield of the Far Future" (copyright 1920 by The Macmillan Company, 1948 by Elizabeth C. Lindsay); from *Collected Poems* by John Masefield: "Wherever Beauty has been Quick in Clay" and 30 lines from untitled Sonnets (copyright 1916, 1944 by John Masefield); "On Growing Old," "A Creed," and "Only a Beauty" (copyright 1912, 1940 by John Masefield); 14 lines from "Lollingdon Downs" (copyright 1930, 1958 by John Masefield); "Glass Houses" from *Collected Poems* by Edwin Arlington Robinson (copyright 1925 by The Macmillan Company, 1948 by Ruth Nivison); "Out of Wisdom, Love," 18 lines from *The Three Taverns* by Edwin Arlington Robinson (copyright 1922 by The Macmillan Company, 1948 by Ruth Nivison); "Yours is the Light" from *Fruit Gathering* by Rabindranath Tagore (copyright 1916 by The Macmillan Company, 1944 by Rathindrinath Tagore); "Prayer for Strength" and "Let This be My Parting Word" from *Gitanjali* by Rabindranath Tagore (copyright 1918 by The Macmillan Company, 1946 by Rathindrinath Tagore); for "All That was Mortal" and "Grace before Sleep" from *Collected Poems* by Sara Teasdale (copyright 1933 by The Macmillan Company); "Stars" from *Collected Poems* by Sara Teasdale (copyright 1920 by The Macmillan Company, 1948 by Mamie T. Wheless); "Ceremony for Birth and Naming" from *Poems* by Ridgely Torrence (copyright 1941 by The Macmillan Company); "Prayer for My Daughter" and "The Second Coming" from *Collected Poems* by William Butler Yeats (copyright 1924 by The Macmillan Company, 1952 by Bertha Georgie Yeats); "Mohini Chatterjee" from *Collected Poems* by William Butler Yeats (copyright 1935 by The Macmillan Company, 1961 by Bertha Georgie

Yeats); "The Four Ages of Man" from *Collected Poems* by William Butler Yeats (copyright 1935 by The Macmillan Company); "Sailing to Byzantium" from *Collected Poems* by William Butler Yeats (copyright 1928 by The Macmillan Company, 1956 by Bertha Georgie Yeats).

VIRGIL MARKHAM for "Man-Test" from *The Shoes of Happiness and Other Poems* by Edwin Markham.

EARL MARLATT for "Pax Nobiscum," "Peter," "Malachi," and "Zechariah" from *Cathedral* (published by Harper & Brothers, copyright 1937 by Earl Marlatt).

NEW DIRECTIONS, New York, for "You, Neighbor God" from *Poems from the Book of Hours*, tr. by Babette Deutsch (copyright 1941 by New Directions); "At a Calvary Near the Ancre" from *The Poems of Wilfred Owen* (all rights reserved); "In the Beginning," "And Death Shall Have No Dominion," and "The Hand that Signed the Paper" from *Collected Poems* by Dylan Thomas (copyright 1957 by New Directions); "Ballad of the Trial of Sodom" and "A Prayer" from *The Death Bell* by Vernon Watkins (copyright 1954 by New Directions); "Psalm" by M. Mendes, tr. by Dudley Poore, "Weeping and Singing" by Cesar Tiempe, tr. by D. D. Walsh, and "The Unforeseen" by C. N. Roxlo, tr. by M. B. Davis, from *An Anthology of Latin-American Poetry* edited by Dudley Fitts (copyright 1942, 1947 by New Directions); "Starlight Like Intuition Pierced the Twelve" from *In Dreams Begin Responsibilities* by Delmore Schwartz (copyright 1938 by New Directions); "Christ Climbed Down" from *A Coney Island of the Mind* by Lawrence Ferlinghetti (copyright 1955, 1958 by Lawrence Ferlinghetti); "The Gift" from *Pictures from Brueghel* by William Carlos Williams (copyright 1962 by William Carlos Williams).

W. W. NORTON & COMPANY, INC., New York, for "Adam," "Eve," "Birth of Mary," "Joseph's Suspicion," "Birth of Christ," "The Garden of Gethsemane," and "The Last Supper" from *Translations from the Poetry of Rainer Maria Rilke* by M. D. Herter Norton (copyright 1938 by W. W. Norton & Company, Inc.); "The Work of Happiness" from *Cloud, Stone, Sun, Vine* by May Sarton (copyright 1961 by May Sarton).

IVAN OBELENSKY, INC., New York, for "Divine Poem: 45" and "Divine Poem: 74" from *Selected Poems and New* by José Garcia Villa.

OXFORD UNIVERSITY PRESS, INC., New York, for "Stone Too Can Pray" from *Collected Poems 1953* by Conrad Aiken (copyright 1953 by Conrad Aiken); "God's Grandeur," "Pied Beauty," and "As Kingfishers Catch Fire" from *Poems of Gerard Manley Hopkins*, Third Edition, edited by W. H. Gardner (copyright 1948 by Oxford University Press, Inc.).

EDITH LOVEJOY PIERCE, for "Remember Thy Covenant," "On Christmas Eve," and "Apocalypse" from *In This Our Day* by Edith Lovejoy Pierce (Harper & Brothers, publishers, copyright Edith Lovejoy Pierce); "The Third Day" from *Therefore Choose Life* (Harper & Brothers, publishers, copyright Edith Lovejoy Pierce).

LAURENCE POLLINGER, LTD., London, for "The Man without Faith" and "Something in Common" from *Collected Poems* by Richard Church.

G. P. PUTNAM'S SONS, New York, for "Easter Hymn" and "To J. S. Bach" from *The Jervis Bay and Other Poems* by Michael Thwaites (copyright 1942 by Michael Thwaites).

RANDOM HOUSE, INC. AND ALFRED A. KNOPF, INC. for "The Unknown Citizen" from Collected Poetry by W. H. Auden (copyright 1940 by W. H. Auden); 32 lines from "For the Time Being" from Collected Poetry by W. H. Auden (copyright 1944 by W. H. Auden); "The Excesses of God" from Be Angry at the Sun and Other Poems by Robinson Jeffers (copyright 1941 by Robinson Jeffers); "Shine, Republic" from Selected Poetry by Robinson Jeffers (copyright 1934, 1962 by Donnan Jeffers and Garth Jeffers); "The Answer" from Selected Poetry by Robinson Jeffers (copyright 1937 by Random House, Inc.); "Look, How Beautiful" from The Beginning and the End by Robinson Jeffers (copyright 1963 by Donnan Jeffers and Garth Jeffers); "The Alphabet" from Poems of a Jew by Karl Shapiro (copyright 1953 by Karl Shapiro); "I Think Continually of Those" from Collected Poems 1928-1953 by Stephen Spender (copyright 1934, 1961 by Stephen Spender); "The War-God" from Collected Poems 1928-1953 by Stephen Spender (copyright 1942 by Stephen Spender); "A Man-Made World" from Collected Poems 1928-1953 by Stephen Spender (copyright 1949 by Stephen Spender); "The Immortal Spirit" from Collected Poems 1928-1953 (copyright 1949 by Stephen Spender); "Garden of Gethsemane," "Evil Days," and "Magdalene" by Boris Pasternak, tr. by Bernard Guilbert Guerney from Doctor Zhivago (copyright 1958 by Pantheon Books); "Peter and John" and "Address to My Soul" from Collected Poems by Elinor Wylie (copyright 1928 by Alfred A. Knopf, Inc., 1956 by Edwina C. Rubenstein); "This Corruptible" from Collected Poems by Elinor Wylie (copyright 1929 by Afred A. Knopf, Inc., 1957 by Edwina C. Rubenstein); "The Pebble" from Collected Poems by Elinor Wylie (copyright 1932 by Alfred A. Knopf, Inc., 1960 by Edwina C. Rubenstein); "The Most Sacred Mountain" from Profiles from China by Eunice Tietjens (copyright 1917 by Alfred A. Knopf, Inc.).

RUSSELL & VOLKENING, INC., NEW York, for "New Year Wishes," "The White-Haired Man," and "Song" from The Lion and the Rose by May Sarton (copyright 1948 by May Sarton).

CHARLES SCRIBNER'S SONS, New York, for "Autumnal" (first published in The New Yorker), "Coming Home," and "Meditation" from Poems Collected and New by Rolfe Humphries (copyright 1946, 1944, 1947 by Rolfe Humphries, 1944 by Charles Scribner's Sons); "The Gift to be Simple" from A Swimmer in the Air by Howard Moss (copyright 1957 by Howard Moss); "Earth," "Golgotha," stanzas from "The Holy Earth," "Unison," and "It is Finished" from Poems Old and New by John Hall Wheelock (copyright 1956 by John Hall Wheelock).

SIDGWICK & JACKSON, LTD., London, for "The Foundation of Faith" and "The Plea" from Collected Poems by John Drinkwater.

SIMON & SCHUSTER, INC., New York, for "The Betrayal," "The Quiet Flower," "The Temple," and "In This Hour" from Year's End by Josephine W. Johnson (copyright 1937 by Josephine W. Johnson); "Are You Born" from One Life by Muriel Rukeyser.

THE SOCIETY OF AUTHORS, London, for "The Scribe" from Collected Poems by Walter de la Mare (permission granted by the Literary Trustees of Walter de la Mare and the Society of Authors as their representative).

THE TALBOT PRESS, LTD., Dublin, for "I See His Blood upon the Rose" by Joseph Plunkett.

TWAYNE PUBLISHERS, INC., New York, for "Testament" from *Address to the Living* by John Holmes (copyright 1937 by John Holmes); "The First Autumn" by Marshall Schacht (copyright 1949 by Marshall Schacht).

THE VIKING PRESS, New York, for "All-Souls' Day," "Asking for It," "Litany of the Lost," "A Midnight Interior," "Strangeness of Heart" from *Collected Poems* by Siegfried Sassoon (all rights reserved); "December Stillness" and "Babylon" from *Collected Poems* by Siegfried Sassoon (copyright 1936 by Siegfried Sassoon); "Evil is Homeless," "The Hands of God," "God and the Holy Ghost," and "When Satan Fell" from *Last Poems* by D. H. Lawrence (copyright 1933 by Frieda Lawrence).

A. P. WATT & SON, London, for "The Beatific Vision," "Femina Contra Mundum," and "The Holy of Holies" from *The Wild Knight and Other Poems* by G. K. Chesterton (also to Miss D. E. Collins, executrix, and Messrs. J. M. Dent & Son, Ltd.).

MARIE DE L. WELCH for "Saint Francis and the Cloud" by Marie De L. Welch (first published in *The Atlantic Monthly*, copyright by Marie De L. Welch).

OSCAR WILLIAMS for "Chant" and "The Last Supper" from *Selected Poems* by Oscar Williams, published by Charles Scribner's Sons and Clarke & Way (copyright 1947 by Oscar Williams); "With God Conversing" by Gene Derwood (copyright by Oscar Williams).

YALE UNIVERSITY PRESS for "For My People," a poem from the book *For My People* by Margaret Walker published by the Yale University Press.

contents

I. PRAISE
"i thank You God"

II. THE IMMENSE CATHEDRAL OF THE HOLY EARTH
"Wherever beauty has been quick in clay"

III. PRAYERS
"But which it only needs that we fulfil"

IV. PEOPLE OF THE BOOK
"When Moses came down from the mountain"

V. NATIVITY
"The stars shall bend their voices,
And every stone shall cry"

VI. HOLY WEEK, EASTER
"I shall descend into my grave,
And on the third day rise again"

VII. THE GOD OF GALAXIES
"O Light Invisible, we praise thee!"

VIII. BROTHERS
"Stranger, may I button-hole you?"

IX. THE HEROIC IN MAN
"I think continually of those who were truly great"

X. THE WAR GOD
"Let law be father of our peace"

XI. THE CHURCH
"around me surges a miracle of unceasing birth and glory and death and resurrection"

XII. DOUBT, SATAN, AND SIN

"Sir, I commend to you the spirit of Lucifer"

XIII. IN THIS HOUR

"Auguries of self-annihilation loom"

XIV.   VISION, THE INTERIOR LIFE

"In certain minds the strength wells
In richness from subterranean springs"

XV.   MORTALITY

"Think, Man of Flesh, and be not proud"

XVI.   TRANSCENDENCE
"Men dance on deathless feet"

fOREWORD

This collection of religious poems, nearly all from the twentieth century, grew from the editor's desire to have the living, contemporary voice of poetry heard from the lectern of his church, alongside great Biblical and non-Biblical poems of the past. All of the poets here represented were born in or lived into this century, with three exceptions. These were Walt Whitman (1819–1892), who came into his own among the poets of our century; Emily Dickinson (1830–1886) and Gerard Manley Hopkins (1844–1889), both of whom were essentially twentieth-century discoveries.

The poets are British and American, although a few neighbors have been "invited in" by way of translations because their poems fit so well into the scheme of this book.

Poetry and religion have always been closely allied. Said Wallace Stephens of the human imagination:

> *I am the necessary angel of earth,*
> *Since in my sight, you see the earth again.*

Imagination is also the necessary angel of the religions. No one of them could have come into existence, or achieved grandeur and significance, without it. The Rig-Veda and the Hebrew Psalms contain poems that will be part of the great tradition of mankind always.

Poetry and religion sometimes speak with one voice. The "imaginative compassion" which Thomas Hardy mentions in one of his prefaces, and which speaks in so many of his poems, is of the essence of both.

Both rejoice in the beauty and majesty of Creation. "Resonance to the all," said Pierre Teilhard de Chardin, "is the keynote of pure religion and of pure poetry."

Both keep themselves open to the mystery. The word "reverence" means literally to fear again, or to stand in awe of once more, as though referring to a second experience—the original experience reflected upon, as in a poem. Poetry, next to great music, best expresses man's sense of the numinous, the ineffable.

Robert Frost once said that one can be poetic about science but not scientific about poetry. So, too, it is possible to be religious about science but not to be scientific about religion. Poetry at its best is not didactic;

where it really communicates it stirs within the reader or the listener an inward response, a music of meaning, similar to that which set the poet singing. Religion at its most effective is not didactic: it communicates a living impulse, "a winged how," from person to person.

That there should be so many poems of praise and prayer as are here included, so many poems with Biblical themes among contemporary poets, so many poems of the Christian year and of the paradigmatic figure of the Son of Man, so many poems of human brotherhood and of profoundly religious questioning and realization, may surprise the reader as it surprised even one who had long been on the lookout for them. Many poets of our time have returned to the spiritual quest, after responding, some of them, to the lure of Marxism and its word "comrade," or wandering in a wilderness of bitter disillusionment.

The progress from nineteenth-century romanticism and optimism to the soberer second thought of today, the breaking up of the older molds into free verse and then the return with a difference to more disciplined forms, tell much of what has happened also in religion. In *The Wasteland*, the most discussed poem of our time, T. S. Eliot spoke for a generation of empty persons lost in a spiritual desert with no springs of living water. Thence, by way of *The Hollow Men*, by way of *The Rock*, a pageant of the Church, and by way of *Ash Wednesday*, a poem of repentance and of spiritual self-searching, he came to the *Four Quartets*, one of the great religious poems of all time.

It would have been good to include the latter, and many others I might mention. But space and cost impose their disciplines. An anthology is necessarily selective. This determines its character, its uniqueness, its capacity to instruct and delight. Perhaps also, it sends the reader ranging further.

J. T.

1   PRAISE

"i thank You God"

1.   i thank You God

i thank You God for most this amazing
day: for the leaping greenly spirits of trees
and a blue true dream of sky; and for everything
which is natural which is infinite which is yes

(i who have died am alive again today,
and this is the sun's birthday; this is the birth
day of life and of love and wings: and of the gay
great happening illimitably earth)

how should tasting touching hearing seeing
breathing any—lifted from the no
of all nothing—human merely being
doubt unimaginable You?

(now the ears of my ears awake and
now the eyes of my eyes are opened)

e e cummings

2.   GOD'S GRANDEUR

The world is charged with the grandeur of God,
    It will flame out, like shining from shook foil;
    It gathers to a greatness, like the ooze of oil
Crushed. Why do men then now not reck his rod?
Generations have trod, have trod, have trod;
    And all is seared with trade; bleared, smeared with toil;
    And wears man's smudge and shares man's smell: the soil
Is bare now, nor can foot feel, being shod.

And for all this, nature is never spent;
    There lives the dearest freshness deep down things;
And though the last lights off the black West went
    Oh, morning, at the brown brink eastward, springs—

Because the Holy Ghost over the bent
World broods with warm breast and with ah! bright wings.

Gerard Manley Hopkins

3.   STONE TOO CAN PRAY

Lord, Lord—these miracles, the streets, all say—
bring to us soon thy best, most golden day,
that every stick and stone for thee may shine,
thy praise be sung in every shaft and line.

Lord, Lord—the steeples and the towers cry—
deepen beyond belief thy ancient sky,
deeper than time or terror be that blue
and we'll still praise thee by still pointing true.

Lord, Lord—the fountains weep—hear our delight,
these waters for birds and children we keep bright;
where children shout, and the stone dolphin sings,
bless with thy rainbow these holy eyes and wings.

Lord, Lord—all voices say, and all together,
stone, steel, and waking man, and waking weather—
give us thy day, that once more we may be
the endless miracle that embodies thee.

Conrad Aiken

4.   A GREETING

Good morning, Life—and all
Things glad and beautiful.
But he that owns the gold,
The Sun, is my great friend—
His spending has no end.
My pockets nothing hold,

Hail to the morning sky,
Which bright clouds measure high;
Hail to you birds whose throats
Would number leaves by notes;
Hail to you shady bowers,
And you green fields of flowers.

Hail to you women fair,
That make a show so rare
In cloth as white as milk—
Be't calico or silk:
Good morning, Life—and all
Things glad and beautiful.

W. H. Davies

5.   THE SCRIBE

What lovely things
    Thy hand hath made:
The smooth-plumed bird
    In its emerald shade,
The seed of the grass,
    The speck of stone
Which the wayfaring ant
    Stirs—and hastes on!
Though I should sit
    By some tarn in thy hills,
Using its ink
    As the spirit wills
To write of Earth's wonders,
    Its live, willed things,
Flit would the ages
    On soundless wings,
Ere unto Z
    My pen drew nigh;
Leviathan told,
    And the honey-fly:

And still would remain
  My wit to try—
My worn reeds broken,
  The dark tarn dry,
All words forgotten—
  Thou, Lord, and I.

Walter de la Mare

6. THE FIRST AUTUMN

Where God had walked
The goldenrod
Sprang like fire
From the burning sod.

The purple asters,
When He spoke,
Rose up beautifully
Like smoke,

And shouting glory
To the sky,
The maple trees
Where He passed by!

But when God blessed
The last bright hill
The holy word
Grew white and still.

Marshall Schacht

7. PIED BEAUTY

Glory be to God for dappled things—
  For skies of couple-colour as a brindled cow;
    For rose-moles all in stipple upon trout that swim;

Fresh-firecoal chestnut falls; finches' wings;
 Landscape plotted and pieced—fold, fallow, and plough;
  And all trades, their gear and tackle and trim.

All things counter, original, spare, strange;
 Whatever is fickle, freckled (who knows how?)
  With swift, slow; sweet, sour; adazzle, dim;
He fathers-forth whose beauty is past change:
 Praise him.

Gerard Manley Hopkins

8.   GOD'S WORLD

O world, I cannot hold thee close enough!
  Thy winds, thy wide grey skies!
  Thy mists, that roll and rise!
Thy woods, this autumn day, that ache and sag
And all but cry with colour! That gaunt crag
To crush! To lift the lean of that black bluff!
World, world, I cannot get thee close enough!

Long have I known a glory in it all,
  But never knew I this:
  Here such a passion is
As stretcheth me apart,—Lord, I do fear
Thou'st made the world too beautiful this year;
My soul is all but out of me,—let fall
No burning leaf; prithee, let no bird call.

Edna St. Vincent Millay

9.   VENI CREATOR

I

Lord of the grass and hill,
Lord of the rain,

White Overlord of will,
Master of pain,

I who am dust and air
Blown through the halls of death,
Like a pale ghost of prayer,—
I am thy breath.

Lord of the blade and leaf,
Lord of the bloom,
Sheer Overlord of grief,
Master of doom,

Lonely as wind or snow,
Through the vague world and dim,
Vagrant and glad I go;
I am thy whim.

Lord of the storm and lull,
Lord of the sea,
I am thy broken gull,
Blown far alee.

Lord of the harvest dew,
Lord of the dawn,
Star of the paling blue
Darkling and gone,

Lost on the mountain height
Where the first winds are stirred,
Out of the wells of night
I am thy word.

Lord of the haunted hush,
Where raptures throng,
I am thy hermit thrush
Ending no song.

Lord of the frost and cold,
Lord of the North,
When the red sun grows old
And day goes forth,

I shall put off this girth,—
Go glad and free,
Earth to my mother earth,
Spirit to thee.

II

Lord of my heart's elation,
Spirit of things unseen,
Be thou my aspiration
Consuming and serene!

Bear up, bear out, bear onward
This mortal self alone,
To selfhood or oblivion,
Incredibly thine own,—

As the foamheads are loosened
And blown along the sea,
Or sink and merge forever
In that which bids them be.

I, too, must climb in wonder,
Uplift at thy command,—
Be one with my frail fellows
Beneath the wind's strong hand,

A fleet and shadowy column
Of dust or mountain rain,
To walk the earth a moment
And be dissolved again.

Be thou my exaltation
Or fortitude of mien,
Lord of the world's elation,
Thou breath of things unseen!

Bliss Carman

10. BREAD THE HOLY

I break my bread. There are the great gold fields
And there the men move with the swaying scythes,
Their wet clothes modelled to their thick slow limbs
Leaving behind them a straight shining path
Where the boys work with knots of stooping women
Binding the sheaves and piling them in place
Like praying hands beneath the summer sky.
Horses unharnessed stand beside their carts
Stamping the flies; a dog lies fast asleep
In hedgerow shadows; now and then a voice
Comes from the gleaners, wells up, murmurs, flows
Into the eddying silence, while above
Silently, slowly, the great clouds are piled
In pale straw-colored mows against the blue.

Elizabeth J. Coatsworth

11. JOHNNY APPLESEED'S HYMN
TO THE SUN

Christ the dew in the clod,
   Christ the sap of the trees,
Christ the light in the waterfall,
   Christ the soul of the sun,
Innermost blood of the sun,
   Grant I may touch the fringes
Of the outermost robe of the sun;

Let me store your rays till my ribs
Carry the breath of lightning,
    Till my lips speak the fulness of thunder
To waken world-weary men:
    Till my whisper engenders lions
Out of the desert weeds.

Give me your eyes, O sun,
    To watch through the universe
Where other suns speed on,
    Brothers, children of God,
Making the great deeps fair.

Take me unto yourself.
    My flesh is a sacrifice,
If only my soul may go
    As a flame to the edge of the sky
Where the sin-born stars come forth
    From the black strong chaos-sea,
From the infinite widths of night.

Grant that I may die in a star
    As the chosen of God all die
Rising again in the dreams
    Of sinning, star born men,
Destroying their sins forever.

Give me your hidden wings,
    That I may go to the heights
Of the gold-built cliffs of heaven,
    Where jungles in silence reign.
Where the streets, knee-deep in moss
    And the mansions heavy with trees
With Cedars of Lebanon
    With olive and orange and palm
Are silent but for the wind,
    Empty, mysterious.

Give me your strength, O sun!
  Give me your hidden wings,
Till I climb to the holiest place,
  That highest plain of all,
With its glassy shallow pools,
  That desert of level fear
Where three great thrones stand high
  Hewn from three ancient mountains,
Blind thrones of a fair lost land.
  You have left your thrones for the suns,
Great God, O Trinity,
  With all your marvelous hosts,
Cherubim, seraphim,
  You blaze in our eyes by day.
They gleam from the stars by night.

Give us your life, O sun!
  Body and blood of Christ,
Wafer of awful fire
  Give us the contrite heart,
Take out the death from us.

Either the dead are dead,
  Or today is eternity,
Your face is eternity,
  Your rays are our endless life.
You are girt with a golden girdle,
  You are with all your crucified
Angels and saints and men
  Who die under clouds in the stars:
You are bringing them back from the dead.
  They breathe on my face as I pray.

Give me your innermost life.
  Come quickly, Alpha, Omega,
Our God, the beginning and end!
                              Vachel Lindsay

12.   YOU

I went into the fields, but you were there
Waiting for me, so all the summer flowers
Were only glimpses of your starry powers;
Beautiful and inspired dust they were.

I went down by the waters, and a bird
Sang with your voice in all the unknown tones
Of all that self of you I have not heard,
So that my being felt you to the bones.

I went into the house, and shut the door
To be alone, but you were there with me;
All beauty in a little room may be,
Though the roof lean and muddy be the floor.

Then in my bed I bound my tired eyes
To make a darkness for my weary brain;
But like a presence you were there again,
Being and real, beautiful and wise. . . .

⌗

The little robin hopping in the wood
Draws friendship from you, the rapt nightingale
Making the night a marvellous solitude,
Only of you to darkness tells the tale.

Kingfishers are but jewels on your dress,
Dun deer that rove and timid rabbits shy
Are but the hintings of your gentleness.
Upon your wings the eagle climbs the sky.

Fish that are shadows in the water pass
With mystery from you, the purpled moth
Dust from your kirtle on his broidery has,
Out of your bounty every beauty floweth.

For you are all, all fire, all living form,
Marvel in man and glory in the worm.

                                        John Masefield

13.   YOURS

Yours is the light that breaks forth from the dark,
and the good that sprouts from the cleft heart of strife.
Yours is the house that opens upon the world, and the
love that calls to the battlefield.
Yours is the gift that still is a gain when everything
is a loss, and the life that flows through the caverns of death.
Yours is the heaven that lies in the common dust,
and you are there for me, you are there for all.

                                        Rabindranath Tagore

14.   NEVER ANOTHER

Praise Him who makes us happy
When not another would;
There is so little reason
In our so little good.

Praise Him who waits all morning,
All afternoon, all night,
All year until this moment
Of that arriving light;

Praise Him who sends it dancing,
Praise Him who lets us see,
And move with it, and listen,
And sing, soberly.

Praise Him who when we lose it
And twilight thickens round,

Remembers where we slumber;
Marks this nether ground;

And waits upon our waking
As never another would;
Praise Him who is the reason,
Praise Him, the only good.

                    Mark Van Doren

15.   CHANT

As God claps hands of time and space
The leaves in millions fall in place
The land becomes by flowers refined
A shade around the flame of mind
And lovers figure in the park
And gravestones settle in the dark
But kingdom go or kingdom come
Rejoicing is where we are from

The sun burns free of might and main
In that far realm beyond the rain
But like a hand in agony bound
The root unclenches in the ground
And millions catch the sun's great eye
And millions hold with roots to die
But kingdom womb or kingdom tomb
Rejoicing is where we are from

The midnight long the sharp stars put
Their blistered lips against our thought
The loving profile of that sleep
Talks with a voice a lifetime deep
And yet the morning on our eyes
Lays the twin flower of the skies
As from a festival we come
Rejoicing is where we are from

Though paradoxes live in words
And facts stampede in frightened herds
A glory beats its feathery shades
Like wings behind our shoulder blades
And lifts us swiftly on the earth
As if still on our way from birth
O now until millennium
Rejoicing is where we are from

Oscar Williams

16. AT A SOLEMN MUSICK

Let the musicians begin,
Let every instrument awaken and instruct us
In love's willing river and love's dear discipline:
We wait, silent, in consent and in the penance
Of patience, awaiting the serene exaltation
Which is the liberation and conclusion of expiation.

Now may the chief musician say:
"Lust and emulation have dwelt among us
Like barbarous kings: have conquered us:
Have inhabited our hearts: devoured and ravished
—With the savage greed and avarice of fire—
The substance of pity and compassion."

Now may all the players play:
"The river of the morning, the morning of the river
Flow out of the splendor of the tenderness of surrender."

Now may the chief musician say:
"Nothing is more important than summer."

And now the entire choir shall chant:
"How often the astonished heart,

Beholding the laurel,
Remembers the dead,
And the enchanted absolute,
Snow's kingdom, sleep's dominion."

Then shall the chief musician declare:
"The phoenix is the meaning of the fruit,
Until the dream is knowledge and knowledge is a dream."

And then, once again, the entire choir shall cry, in passionate unity,
Singing and celebrating love and love's victory,
Ascending and descending the heights of assent, climbing and chant-
                                            ing triumphantly:
Before the morning was, you were:
Before the snow shone,
And the light sang, and the stone,
Abiding, rode the fullness or endured the emptiness,
You were: you were alone.

                                            Delmore Schwartz

II the immense cathedral
of the holy earth

"Wherever beauty has been quick in clay"

17. THIS FEVERS ME

This fevers me, this sun on green,
On grass glowing, this young spring.
The secret hallowing is come,
Regenerate sudden incarnation,
Mystery made visible
In growth, yet subtly veiled in all,
Unundertandable in grass,
In flowers, and in the human heart,
This lyric mortal loveliness,
The earth breathing, and the sun.
The young lambs sport, none udderless.
Rabbits dash beneath the brush.
Crocuses have come; wind flowers
Tremble against quick April.
Violets put on the night's blue,
Primroses wear the pale dawn,
The gold daffodils have stolen
From the sun. New grass leaps up;
Gorse yellows, starred with day;
The willow is a graceful dancer
Poised; the poplar poises too.
The apple takes the seafoam's light,
And the evergreen tree is densely bright.
April, April, when will he
Be gaunt, be old, who is so young?
This fevers me, this sun on green,
On grass glowing, this young spring.

Richard Eberhart

18. IN THE IMMENSE CATHEDRAL

from "The Holy Earth"

In the immense cathedral of the holy earth,
Whose arches are the heavens and the great vault above,

Groined with its myriad stars, what miracles of birth,
What sacraments of death, what rituals of love!

Her nave is the wide world and the whole length of it,
One flame on all her altars kindles her many fires;
Wherever the clear tapers of trembling life are lit
Resound for joy the old, indomitable choirs.

The holy church of earth with clamorous worshippers
Is crowded, and fierce hungers, faithful every onc
To the one faith; that stern and simple faith of hers
Contents the heart that asks no pity, giving none.

Each on the other feeds, and all on each are fed,
And each for all is offered—a living offering, where
In agony and triumph the ancient feast is spread,
Life's sacramental supper, that all her sons may share.

They mingle with one another, blend—mingle—merge, and flow
Body into wild body; in rapture endlessly
Weaving, with intricate motions of being, to and fro,
The pattern of all Being, one mighty harmony:

One Body, of all bodies woven and interwrought—
One Self, in many selves, through their communion
In love and death, made perfect, wherein each self is nought
Save as it serve the many, mysteriously made One.

                                        John Hall Wheelock

19.   MIRACLES

Why! who makes much of a miracle?
As to me, I know of nothing else but miracles,
Whether I walk the streets of Manhattan,
Or dart my sight over the roofs of houses toward the sky,
Or wade with naked feet along the beach, just in the edge of the
                                                    water,

Or stand under trees in the woods,
Or talk by day with any one I love—or sleep in the bed at night with
                                        any one I love,

Or sit at table at dinner with my mother,
Or look at strangers opposite me riding in the car,
Or watch honey-bees busy around the hive, of a summer forenoon,
Or animals feeding in the fields,
Or birds—or the wonderfulness of insects in the air,
Or the wonderfulness of the sun-down—or of stars shining so quiet
                                        and bright,
Or the exquisite, delicate, thin curve of the new moon in spring;
Or whether I go among those I like best, and that like me best—
                                        mechanics, boatmen, farmers,
Or among the savants—or to the soiree—or to the opera,
Or stand a long while looking at the movements of machinery,
Or behold children at their sports,
Or the admirable sight of the perfect old man, or the perfect old
                                        woman,
Or the sick in hospitals, or the dead carried to burial,
Or my own eyes and figure in the glass;
These, with the rest, one and all, are to me miracles,
The whole referring—yet each distinct, and in its place.

To me, every hour of the light and dark is a miracle,
Every cubic inch of space is a miracle,
Every square yard of the surface of the earth is spread with the same,
Every foot of the interior swarms with the same;
Every spear of grass—the frames, limbs, organs, of men and women,
                                        and all that concerns them,
All these to me are unspeakably perfect miracles.

To me the sea is a continual miracle;
The fishes that swim—the rocks—the motions of the waves—the
                                        ships, with men in them,
What stranger miracles are there?

                                        Walt Whitman

20.   WHEREVER BEAUTY HAS BEEN QUICK IN CLAY

Wherever beauty has been quick in clay
Some effluence of it lives, a spirit dwells,
Beauty that death can never take away,
Mixed with the air that shakes the flower bells;

So that by waters where the apples fall,
Or in lone glens, or valleys full of flowers,
Or in the streets where bloody tidings call,
The haunting waits the mood that makes it ours.

Then at a turn, a word, an act, a thought,
Such difference comes, the spirit apprehends
That place's glory, for where beauty fought
Under the veil the glory never ends,

But the still grass, the leaves, the trembling flower
Keep, through dead time, that everlasting hour.

                                          John Masefield

21.   HOW MANY HEAVENS . . .

The emeralds are singing on the grasses,
And in the trees the bells of the long cold are ringing—
My blood seems changed to emeralds like the spears
Of grass beneath the earth piercing and singing.

The flame of the first blade
Is an angel piercing through the earth to sing
'God is everything!
The grass within the grass, the angel in the angel, flame
Within the flame, and He is the green shade that came
To be the heart of shade.'

The gray-beard angel of the stone,
Who has grown wise with age, cried, 'Not alone
Am I within my silence—God is the stone in the still stone, the
                                                    silence laid
In the heart of silence' . . . then, above the glade,

The yellow straws of light,
Whereof the sun has built his nest, cry 'Bright
Is the world, the yellow straw
My brother—God is the straw within the straw: —All things are
                                                            Light.'

He is the sea of ripeness and the sweet apple's emerald lore.
So you, my flame of grass, my root of the world from which all Spring
                                                    shall grow,
O you, my hawthorn bough of the stars, now leaning low
Through the day, for your flowers to kiss my lips, shall know
He is the core of the heart of love, and He, beyond laboring seas, our
                                                    ultimate shore.

Edith Sitwell

22.   EARTH

Grasshopper, your tiny song
And my poem alike belong
To the dark and silent earth,
From which all poetry has birth;
All we say and all we sing
Is but as the murmuring
Of that drowsy heart of hers
When from her deep dream she stirs:
If we sorrow, or rejoice,
You and I are but her voice.

Deftly does the dust express,
In mind, her hidden loveliness—
And, from her cool silence, stream
The cricket's cry and Dante's dream;

For the earth, that breeds the trees,
Breeds cities too, and symphonies,
Equally her beauty flows
Into a savior, or a rose—
Looks down in dream, and from above
Smiles at herself in Jesus' love;
Christ's love and Homer's art
Are but the workings of her heart,
Through Leonardo's hand she seeks
Herself, and through Beethoven speaks
In holy thunderings that sound
The awful message of the ground.

The serene and humble mold
Does in herself all selves enfold,
Kingdoms, destinies, and creeds,
Proud dreams, heroic deeds,
Science, that probes the firmament,
The high, inflexible intent
Of one, for many, sacrificed;
Plato's brain, the heart of Christ,
All love, all legend, and all lore
Are in the dust forevermore.

Even as the growing grass,
Up from the soil religions pass,
And the field that bears the rye
Bears parables and prophecy—
Out of the earth the poem grows,
Like the lily, or the rose;
And all man is, or yet may be,
Is but herself in agony
Toiling up the steep ascent
Toward the complete accomplishment
When all dust shall be—the whole
Universe—one conscious soul.
Yea, the quiet and cool sod
Bears in her breast the dream of God.

If you would know what earth is, scan
The intricate, proud heart of man,
Which is the earth articulate,
And learn how holy and how great,
How limitless, and how profound,
Is the nature of the ground—
How without question or demur,
We may entrust ourselves to her
When we are wearied out and lay
Our bodies in the common clay.

For she is pity, she is love,
All wisdom, she, all thoughts that move
About her everlasting breast
Till she gathers them to rest—
All tenderness of all the ages,
Seraphic secrets of the sages,
Vision and hope of all the seers,
All prayer, all anguish, and all tears,
Are but the dust, that from her dream
Awakes, and knows herself supreme;
Are but earth, when she reveals
All that her secret heart conceals
Down in the dark and silent loam,
Which is ourselves, asleep, at home.

Yes, and this, my poem, too,
Is part of her as dust and dew—
Wherein herself she doth declare,
Through my lips, and say her prayer.

      John Hall Wheelock

23. THE HOLY OF HOLIES

"Elder father, though thine eyes
Shine with holy mysteries,

Canst thou tell me what in the heart
Of a cowslip blossom lies?

"Smaller than all lives that be,
Secret as the deepest sea,
Stands a little house of seeds,
Like an elfin's granary.

"Speller of the stones and weeds,
Skilled in Nature's crafts and creeds,
Tell me what is in the heart
Of the smallest of the seeds."

"God Almighty, and with Him
Cherubim and Seraphim,
Filling all eternity—
Adonai Elohim."

                    G. K. Chesterton

24.   STARS

Alone in the night
   On a dark hill
With pines around me
   Spicy and still,

And a heaven full of stars
   Over my head,
White and topaz
   And misty red;

Myriads with beating
   Hearts of fire
That aeons
   Cannot vex or tire;

Up the dome of heaven
  Like a great hill,
I watch them marching
  Stately and still,

And I know that I
  Am honored to be
Witness
  Of so much majesty.

                              Sara Teasdale

III   PRAYERS

"But which it only needs that we fulfil"

25.   A PRAYER IN SPRING

Oh, give us pleasure in the flowers to-day;
And give us not to think so far away
As the uncertain harvest; keep us here
All simply in the springing of the year.

Oh, give us pleasure in the orchard white,
Like nothing else by day, like ghosts by night;
And make us happy in the happy bees,
The swarm dilating round the perfect trees.

And make us happy in the darting bird
That suddenly above the bees is heard,
The meteor that thrusts in with needle bill,
And off a blossom in mid air stands still.

For this is love and nothing else is love,
The which it is reserved for God above
To sanctify to what far ends He will,
But which it only needs that we fulfil.

Robert Frost

26.   may my heart always be open

may my heart always be open to little
birds who are the secrets of living
whatever they sing is better than to know
and if men should not hear them men are old

may my mind stroll about hungry
and fearless and thirsty and supple
and even if it's sunday may i be wrong
for whenever men are right they are not young

and may myself do nothing usefully
and love yourself so more than truly

there's never been quite such a fool who could fail
pulling all the sky over him with one smile

e e cummings

27. FOR MY DAUGHTER
From "Prayer for My Daughter"

⊠

May she be granted beauty and yet not
Beauty to make a stranger's eye distraught,
Or hers before a looking-glass, for such,
Being made beautiful overmuch,
Consider beauty a sufficient end,
Lose natural kindness and maybe
The heart-revealing intimacy
That chooses right, and never find a friend.

⊠

In courtesy I'd have her chiefly learned;
Hearts are not had as a gift but hearts are earned
By those that are not entirely beautiful;
Yet many, that have played the fool
For beauty's very self, has charm made wise,
And many a poor man that has roved,
Loved and thought himself beloved,
From a glad kindness cannot take his eyes.

May she become a flourishing hidden tree
That all her thoughts may like the linnet be,
And have no business but dispensing round
Their magnanimities of sound,
Nor but in merriment begin a chase,
Nor but in merriment a quarrel.
O may she live like some green laurel
Rooted in one dear perpetual place.

My mind, because the minds that I have loved,
The sort of beauty that I have approved,
Prosper but little, has dried up of late,
Yet knows that to be choked with hate
May well be of all evil chances chief.
If there's no hatred in a mind
Assault and battery of the wind
Can never tear the linnet from the leaf.

⊠

Considering that, all hatred driven hence,
The soul recovers radical innocence
And learns at last that it is self-delighting,
Self-appeasing, self-affrighting,
And that its own sweet will is Heaven's will;
She can, though every face should scowl
And every windy quarter howl
Or every bellows burst, be happy still.

And may her bridegroom bring her to a house
Where all's accustomed, ceremonious;
For arrogance and hatred are the wares
Peddled in the thoroughfares.
How but in custom and in ceremony
Are innocence and beauty born?
Ceremony's a name for the rich horn,
And custom for the spreading laurel tree.

William Butler Yeats

28.   A PRAYER

If I dare pray for one
Gift in the coming age
That might protect my son
On every shifting stage
Keeping his joy as true
As now he feels in play
Fetching the ball I threw

Or pitched from day to day
Safe in a cot where sleep
Finds him still clasping toys
Until I step and stoop
And loose them with no noise,
I pray that he may have
Recourse in argument
After the falling wave
To what remains unspent,
That he may stoop and dare
To gather for his own
In that loud, hostile air
One word's deliberate throne,
I mean the uncounted praise,
The bridegroom's calm return
For which all night and days
In speculation burn.
There where the breakers fly
Scattering their bridal lace,
Where instantly joy's eye
Rejects the commonplace,
Let him find strength to throw
Compromise to the winds
Though constancy forgo
All but his truest friends,
And patiently repair
The drift of broken vows,
Creating from despair
His Christ-appointed house,
That in the testing hour
Of hostile circumstance
His soul may put on power,
The impotence of chance
Revealing in his hold
On envy's taunting mind
Like Samson, Tranquil-souled,
Who remained strong, though blind.

                                        Vernon Watkins

29.   GRACE BEFORE SLEEP

How can our minds and bodies be
Grateful enough that we have spent
Here in this generous room, we three,
This evening of content?
Each one of us has walked through storm
And fled the wolves along the road;
But here the hearth is wide and warm,
And for this shelter and this light
Accept, O Lord, our thanks to-night.

Sara Teasdale

30.   FOR STRENGTH

This is my prayer to thee, my lord—strike, strike at the root of penury
in my heart.
Give me the strength lightly to bear my joys and sorrows.
Give me the strength never to disown the poor or bend my knees
before insolent might.
Give me the strength to raise my mind high above daily trifles.
And give me strength to surrender my strength to thy will with love.

Rabindranath Tagore

31.   A PRAYER TO GO TO PARADISE
WITH THE DONKEYS

When I must come to you, O my God, I pray
It be some dusty-roaded holiday,
And even as in my travels here below,
I beg to choose by what road I shall go
To Paradise, where the clear stars shine by day.
I'll take my walking-stick and go my way,
And to my friends the donkeys I shall say,
"I am Francis Jammes, and I'm going to Paradise,

For there is no hell in the land of the loving God."
And I'll say to them: "Come, sweet friends of the blue skies,
Poor creatures who with a flap of the ears or a nod
Of the head shake off the buffets, the bees, the flies . . ."

Let me come with these donkeys, Lord, into your land,
These beasts who bow their head so gently, and stand
With their small feet joined together in a fashion
Utterly gentle, asking your compassion.
I shall arrive, followed by their thousands of ears,
Followed by those with baskets at their flanks,
By those who lug the carts of mountebanks
Or loads of feather-dusters and kitchen-wares,
By those with humps of battered water-cans,
By bottle-shaped she-asses who halt and stumble,
By those tricked out in little pantaloons
To cover their wet, blue galls where flies assemble
In whirling swarms, making a drunken hum.

Dear God, let it be with these donkeys that I come,
And let it be that angels lead us in peace
To leafy streams where cherries tremble in air,
Sleek as the laughing flesh of girls; and there
In that haven of souls let it be that, leaning above
Your divine waters, I shall resemble these donkeys,
Whose humble and sweet poverty will appear
Clear in the clearness of your eternal love.

Francis Jammes
tr. *Richard Wilbur*

32.   LET ME ENJOY

I

Let me enjoy the earth no less
Because the all-enacting Might

That fashioned forth its loveliness
Had other aims than my delight.

II

About my path there flits a Fair,
Who throws me not a word or sign;
I'll charm me with her ignoring air,
And laud the lips not meant for mine.

III

From manuscripts of moving song
Inspired by scenes and dreams unknown,
I'll pour out raptures that belong
To others, as they were my own.

IV

And some day hence, towards Paradise
And all its blest—if such should be—
I will lift glad, afar-off eyes,
Though it contain no place for me.

Thomas Hardy

33. THE LEADEN-EYED

Let not young souls be smothered out before
They do quaint deeds and fully flaunt their pride.
It is the world's one crime its babes grow dull,
Its poor are ox-like, limp and leaden-eyed.

Not that they starve, but starve so dreamlessly,
Not that they sow, but that they seldom reap,
Not that they serve, but have no gods to serve,
Not that they die, but that they die like sheep.

Vachel Lindsay

34.   ON GROWING OLD

Be with me, Beauty, for the fire is dying,
My dog and I are old, too old for roving.
Man, whose young passion sets the spindrift flying,
Is soon too lame to march, too cold for loving.
I take the book and gather to the fire,
Turning old yellow leaves; minute by minute,
The clock ticks to my heart; a withered wire
Moves a thin ghost of music in the spinet.
I cannot sail your seas, I cannot wander
Your cornland, nor your hill-land nor your valleys,
Ever again, nor share the battle yonder
Where the young knight the broken squadron rallies.
Only stay quiet while my mind remembers
The beauty of fire from the beauty of embers.

Beauty, have pity, for the strong have power,
The rich their wealth, the beautiful their grace,
Summer of man its sunlight and its flower,
Spring-time of man all April in a face.
Only, as in the jostling in the Strand,
Where the mob thrusts or loiters or is loud,
The beggar with the saucer in his hand
Asks only a penny from the passing crowd,
So, from this glittering world with all its fashion,
Its fire and play of men, its stir, its march,
Let me have wisdom, Beauty, wisdom and passion,
Bread to the soul, rain where the summers parch.
Give me but these, and though the darkness close
Even the night shall blossom as the rose.

John Masefield

35.   A MIDNIGHT INTERIOR

To-night while I was pondering in my chair
I saw for the first time a circle of brightness

Made by my patient lamp up on the ceiling.
It shone like a strange flower; and then my stare
Discovered an arctic snowstorm in that whiteness;
And then some pastoral vale of rayed revealing.

White flowers were in a bowl beside my book;
In midnight's miracle of light they glowed,
And every petal there in silence showed
My life the way to wonder with a look.

O inwardness of trust—intelligence—
Release my soul through every door of sense:
Give me new sight; O grant me strength to find
From lamp and flower simplicity of mind.

Siegfried Sassoon

36.   DROP ME THE SEED

Drop me the seed, that I, even in my brain
May be its nourishing earth. No mortal knows
From what immortal granary comes the grain,
Nor how the earth conspires to make the rose;

But from the dust and from the wetted mud
Comes help, given or taken; so with me
Deep in my brain the essence of my blood
Shall give it stature until Beauty be.

It will look down, even as the burning flower
Smiles upon June, long after I am gone.
Dust-footed Time will never tell its hour,
Through dusty Time its rose will draw men on,

Through dusty Time its beauty shall make plain
Man, and, Without, a spirit scattering grain.

John Masefield

37. THE SWORD OF SURPRISE

Sunder me from my bones, O sword of God,
Till they stand stark and strange as do the trees;
That I whose heart goes up with the soaring woods
May marvel as much at these.

Sunder me from my blood that in the dark
I hear that red ancestral river run,
Like branching buried floods that find the sea
But never see the sun.

Give me miraculous eyes to see my eyes,
Those rolling mirrors made alive in me,
Terrible crystal more incredible
Than all the things they see.

Sunder me from my soul, that I may see
The sins like streaming wounds, the life's brave beat;
Till I shall save myself, as I would save
A stranger in the street.

G. K. Chesterton

38. DECEMBER STILLNESS

December stillness, teach me through your trees
That loom along the west, one with the land,
The veiled evangel of your mysteries.
   While nightfall, sad and spacious, on the down
   Deepens, and dusk imbues me, where I stand,
   With grave diminishings of green and brown,
   Speak, roofless Nature, your instinctive words;
   And let me learn your secret from the sky,
   Following a flock of steadfast, journeying birds
   In lone remote migration beating by.
December stillness, crossed by twilight roads,
Teach me to travel far and bear my loads.

Siegfried Sassoon

39.   THE UNFORESEEN

Lord never grant me what I ask for.
The unforeseen delights me, what comes down
from your fair stars; let life
deal out before me all at once the cards

against which I must play. I want the shock
of going silently along my dark street,
feeling that I am tapped upon the shoulder,
turning about, and seeing the face of adventure.

I do not want to know where and how
I shall meet death. Caught unaware,
may my soul learn at the turn of a corner
that one step back it still lived.

Conrado Nale Roxlo
tr. from the Spanish by
Milton Ben Davis

40.   PRAYER ON THE NIGHT
BEFORE EASTER

My God, whose law I believe in, and have signed to serve in my best,
My voice comes strange to you, and new, and never raised before.
This is the new time, and I have a first prayer to make, addressed
Not so much in jubilation as in need, as the newcomer asks more.

Make my mother's dying easy and soon, and make my son's growing
Long. Give my wife her child. Allow me years enough. And gather
Under your care those I believe You love as I do, not much showing
Love, except in the unspoken ways of being and of coming together.

Heal our illnesses which we have brought upon ourselves. Help us.
I myself have evaded punishment, and have been subtle, and secret.
Lord, do justly what heat, weight, and water do, and star-rise,
Hear me. My beloved trust my trust in You, that You never forget.

I ask too much, stirred who should be stilled by this holiday.
What a beggar! I burst out with my troubles and my crowded love,
Trying to say everything at once. But I was never taught to pray.
Forgive me, and let me help You remember those I am thinking of.

Prisoners of war, the war far away and brutal, or the war near,
Silent and terrible and complicated and within, where wars begin.
I would like to know You know. I think always of someone somewhere
Who cries out to me, and You, and may not be heard, and cries again.

And those with no words, all those with no lucky skill, and no luck.
The twisted. The trapped in small anxieties. The girl with no face
A man will look at. The man who can work, and can find no work.
Lord, think with me, think with me, as I reach to You from this
                                                               place.

My wife carrying our child. I said that. All those separated.
All those who wait. Those, too, who rule themselves, or else rule.
Those leading the way through workings of the law, and those led.
Those lost. The very young. The very old. But I know You know
                                                          them all.

For my kind of selfishness, thank You, that I have been let be
This busy, unadmirable, this persistent, unruly, this same me.
But I will not cancel myself in Your eyes. I must be here.
I must be. And as I can, and with Your consent, I must care.

Thank You for the example of great men to men less known,
And somehow let them know that they stand, and they stand up.
I mean, too, the quiet artists, and doctors, men on their own
Working. Put Your hand under them, that they may not stop,

That they may not fall, that like the force of gravity, You,
Whose hand is under us all, will balance and bear us. And keep
Oh kitchen-and-wood-smell ours, and all we hardly know we do,
And keep for us, those of us who need it, sleep, and sleep.

John Holmes

41.   BENEDICTION

God banish from your house
The fly, the roach, the mouse

That riots in the walls
Until the plaster falls;

Admonish from your door
The hypocrite and liar;

No shy, soft, tigrish fear
Permit upon your stair,

Nor agents of your doubt.
God drive them whistling out.

Let nothing touched with evil,
Let nothing that can shrivel

Heart's tenderest frond, intrude
Upon your still, deep blood.

Against the drip of night
God keep all windows tight,

Protect your mirrors from
Surprise, delirium,

Admit no trailing wind
Into your shuttered mind

To plume the lake of sleep
With dreams. If you must weep

God give you tears, but leave
You secrecy to grieve,

And islands for your pride,
And love to nest in your side.

God grant that, to the bone,
Yourself may be your own;

God grant that I may be
(My sweet) sweet company.

Stanley *Kunitz*

42.   FOR YOU

The peace of great doors be for you.
Wait at the knobs, at the panel oblongs.
Wait for the great hinges.

The peace of great churches be for you,
Where the players of lofty pipe organs
Practice old lovely fragments, alone.

The peace of great books be for you,
Stains of pressed clover leaves on pages,
Bleach of the light of years, held in leather.

The peace of great prairies be for you.
Listen among wind players in cornfields,
The wind leaning over its oldest music.

The peace of great seas be for you.
Wait on a hook of land, a rock footing
For you, wait in the salt wash.

The peace of great mountains be for you,
The sleep and the eyesight of eagles,
Sheet mist shadows and the long look across.

The peace of great silhouettes be for you,
Shadow dancers alive in your blood now,
Alive and crying, "Let us out, let us out."

The peace of great changes be for you.
Whisper, Oh beginners in the hills.
Tumble, Oh cubs—tomorrow belongs to you.

The peace of great loves be for you.
Rain, soak these roots; wind, shatter the dry rot.
Bars of sunlight, grips of the earth, hug these.

The peace of great ghosts be for you,
Phantoms of night-gray eyes, ready to go
To the fog-star dumps, to the fire-white doors.

Yes, the peace of great phantoms be for you,
Phantom iron men, mothers of bronze,
Keepers of the lean clean breeds.

Carl Sandburg

IV   PEOPLE OF THE BOOK

———

"When Moses came down from the mountain"

43. THE ALPHABET

The letters of the Jews as strict as flames
On little terrible flowers lean
Stubbornly upwards through the perfect ages,
Singing through solid stone the sacred names.
The letters of the Jews are black and clean
And lie in chain-line over Christian pages.
The chosen letters bristle like barbed wire
That hedge the flesh of man,
Twisting and tightening the book that warns.
These words, this burning bush, this flickering pyre
Unsacrifices the bled son of man
Yet plaits his crown with thorns.

Where go the tipsy idols of the Roman
Past synagogues of patient time,
Where go the sisters of the Gothic rose,
Where go the blue eyes of the Polish women
Past the almost natural crime,
Past the still speaking embers of ghettos,
There rise the tender flowers of the Jews.
The letters of the Jews are dancing knives
That carve the heart of darkness seven ways.
These are the letters that all men refuse
And will refuse until the king arrives
And will refuse until the death of time
And all is rolled back in the book of days.

Karl Shapiro

44. ADAM

Marveling he stands on the cathedral's
steep ascent, close to the rose window,
as though frightened at the apotheosis
which grew and all at once

set him down over these and these.
And straight he stands and glad of his endurance,
simply determined; as the husbandman
who began and who knew not how

from the garden of Eden finished-full
to find a way out into
the new earth. God was hard to persuade;

and threatened him, instead of acceding,
ever and again, that he would die.
Yet man persisted: she will bring forth.

Rainer Maria Rilke
tr. *from the German by M. D. Herter Norton*

45.   EVE

Simply she stands on the cathedral's
great ascent, close to the rose window,
With the apple in the apple-pose,
guiltless-guilty once and for all

of the growing she gave birth to
since from the circle of eternities
loving she went forth, to struggle through
her way throughout the earth like a young year.

Ah, gladly yet a little in that land
would she have lingered, heeding the harmony
and understanding of the animals.

But since she found the man determined,
she went with him, aspiring after death,
and she had as yet hardly known God.

Rainer Maria Rilke
tr. *from the German by M. D. Herter Norton*

46.   NOAH

"It's going to rain," said Noah. His friend laughed.
  "You're always saying it's going to rain," he said.
"The earth is brick and dust and you talk of a raft.
  You're getting old. There's something loose in your head."

"It's going to rain," said Noah, with bleak eyes
  That saw nothing, not even a friend's disdain.
"It's going to rain, and the rivers are going to rise,
  I don't know when. But it's going, it's going to rain."

"You're drunk," said his friend. "I was, but I'm sober now."
  "You're cracked." "I was, but I seem to have mended my brain.
The times were all wheels and dust, but now, somehow,
  There are no more wheels and the dust is calling the rain.

"It's going to rain. The clouds will come over the peak
  And the dust will run like an antelope over the plain,
And the dark will cover the sun and the wind will speak,
  And drop and drop like thunder will come the rain.

"And the rain will fall and fall, and the waters rise
  And smother the house and the harvest and leave no trace,
And dissolve the mountains themselves before your eyes
  And inch up your body at last and cover your face.

"It's going to rain," said Noah. "I don't know when.
  But it can't be long; the wind has an angry note.
And I'm out to cut some lumber and call my men
  In from the fields to lay me a keel for a boat."

"You are a fool, Noah." "I was a fool.
  I do not feel wise now; only somehow sane.
I have walked alone and gone to the Voice to school
  And I am building a boat against the rain."

"I shan't go build a boat. What if it rain?
  There has been rain before. The waters rose.

The waters fell, the good sun shone again.
　The worst nor'easter has a crimson close."

"There will be sunrise after many days,
　But not for those who build themselves no ark.
The fields will sparkle and the peaks will blaze,
　But not the eyes of drowned men in the dark.

"There will be sunrise and a world to make
　New with remembered lore, and fires to light
From old fires loved and tended for hope's sake;
　But first there will be rain, there will be night.

"Get lumber and build your arks, each to his need!
　Unchain the plough. You will not harvest grain.
It's going to rain," cried Noah. "Won't anyone heed?
　Build you an ark! I tell you, it's going to rain."

Herman Hagedorn

47.　ABRAHAM

　The rivulet-loving wanderer Abraham
　Through waterless wastes tracing his fields of pasture
　Led his Chaldean herds and fattening flocks
　With the meandering art of wavering water
　That seeks and finds, yet does not know its way.
　He came, rested and prospered, and went on,
　Scattering behind him little pastoral kingdoms,
　And over each one its own particular sky,
　Not the great rounded sky through which he journeyed,
　That went with him but when he rested changed.
　His mind was full of names
　Learned from strange peoples speaking alien tongues,
　And all that was theirs one day he would inherit.
　He died content and full of years, though still

The Promise had not come, and left his bones,
Far from his father's house, in alien Canaan.

Edwin Muir

48.   BALLAD OF THE TRIAL OF SODOM

God came to Abram,
Abram the man
Who knew no glory
Could resist God's ban,
And God said: 'Abram,
I come to destroy
Sodom, Sodom,
Sodom, Sodom,
That golden city
Of sin and joy.'

Thunder. Thunder. Thunder. Thunder.
Death is terrible, a thing of wonder.
First is a lethargy that no man likes,
Then comes the moment when the lightning strikes.

Then Abram, trying
To save that place,
Thinking of the dying,
Fell upon his face.
'Lord, if there were fifty
Righteous men
In Sodom, Sodom,
Sodom, Sodom,
Men who were steadfast,
Would you destroy it then?'

Heaven knows what payment
An advocate should ask,
But old man Abram
Had the hardest task.

He looked at Sodom
And he heard God's voice:
'Sodom, Sodom,
Sodom, Sodom;
Hide not the city
That my hand destroys.'

And Abram was trying
To save that place.
He lay for a long time
And could not lift his face.
'White though the lightning
Where the thunder rolls
Towards Sodom, Sodom,
Sodom, Sodom,
I shall not destroy it
If there are fifty souls.'

And Abram pondered.
He could not make amends.
It lightened and thundered.
He counted up his friends.
'Lord God, have patience.
May flesh be left alive
In Sodom, Sodom,
That doomed city,
If the fifty lack five?'

The Lord God darkened
Like a fiery cloud.
Abram waited
As he lay there bowed;
He saw Hell's demons
In a midnight dive
In Sodom, Sodom,
Sodom, Sodom.
'I shall not destroy it
For the forty-and-five.'

'Lord God, have patience.
Destruction is just;
To hide the accursed
In the darkest dust.
But should there be forty
In the temple found
Of Sodom, Sodom,
Sodom, Sodom,
Then would you brand it,
Raze it to the ground?'

Abram breathed.
A long breath he took.
He thought of the temple,
And the temple shook.
Monsters of sacrilege
Sprawled where it stood
In Sodom, Sodom,
Sodom, Sodom.
*I would not brand it
For the forty good.*'

And Abram knew,
Abram knew,
This was the hardest
Peace for which to sue.
'Lord God, forgive me
That I should speak again
Of Sodom, Sodom,
Sodom, Sodom.
Would you spare the city
For thirty good men?'

Thunder. Thunder. Thunder. Thunder.
Death is terrible, a thing of wonder.
First is a lethargy that no man likes,
Then comes the moment when the lightning strikes.

And Abram counted
Try as he would,
He could not make up the number
To thirty good.
The Judgment's answer
Came upon him then:
'Tell Sodom, Sodom,
Sodom, Sodom,
I shall not destroy it
For thirty good men.'

Abram was silent.
Abram was dumb.
He heard Hell's demons
Beating on a drum.
He saw men carried
Under long, slim poles
Through Sodom, Sodom,
Sodom, Sodom,
'Lord, would you save it
For twenty souls?'

This was the last time.
This was the last.
Now for the brimstone
And the blinding blast.
He saw huge darkness
Like a hangman's hood
On Sodom, Sodom,
Sodom, Sodom.
'I still would spare it
For the twenty good.'

'Lord, Thou art just.
Lord, Thou art just.
How should we utter
Who are less than dust?
Yet so wicked

Are the hearts of men
In Sodom, Sodom,
Sodom, Sodom.
Still would you spare it
If the good were ten?'

Fearful the silence,
Fearful the span
Stretching that moment
Between God and man.
Abram sweated
His life out then
For Sodom, Sodom,
Sodom, Sodom.
'I shall not destroy it
If the good are ten.'

Abram the father
Counting up the cost
Saw faith plainly
And knew that he had lost.
God looked at Sodom
In that pleading place,
Sodom, Sodom,
Sodom, Sodom.
Down looked Abram,
And he lost his case.

                                   Vernon Watkins

49.   JACOB AND THE ANGEL

His mother's fondness wrought his father's frown.
Supplanter from the beginning, struggler in the womb,
Heel-holder, the overreaching scion. She egged him on.
For her offense she saw him hounded out of home
Nor lived to look again, ever, on the longed face.

Well warned if rudely, weaned, the outflying son
Beheld the laddered angels in their intercourse with earth,
His first liberating sign, if late. In that deliverance,
Freed from the mother's death-hug, trended east,
And over the well-dark water gazed on the sudden bride.

But guilt had split him. Deep down the offended father
Lived on symbolic in the maid's evasive sire,
His mother's brother. Duped by the blear-eyed sister
In his bed, trickster out-tricked, he swallowed gall,
And suffered the serfdom of those sweat-compounded years.

Suffered and loved and prospered. Even in bondage
His talents stood him well: the slat-eyed ewes
Bred neatly, flocks flourished, his wealth was won.
Seizing his sunk soul force he broke for the border;
Faced out the father on the slope of Galaad.

Faced, forced the offender, and sudden victor, saw
The signifying angels at the Camps of God,
Mark of the second liberation. Father-freed,
He gathered up the measure of his mind, turned home
To offer restitution, expunge the ancient debt.

But fear still fouled him. The raw unreckonable guilt
Sapped at his manhood, guttered his whole-felt strength.
Off there the beaten brother mustered up his men.
How could the exile know but that the wound
Had sown a poison, wrathful, had festered the sullen years?

And falling on his face he prayed to God, and rose
Dividing family from family, setting flock from flock,
Over the ford of Jaboc. Shivering he watched them
Breast the dark water. All was committed now. Alone
He waded the freshet last in the apophatic night.

But hold. Tall by the boulder, athwart the torrential flow
Spied out one shadow menacing that ford.

Esau? Stalking perhaps the hazardous creek-cross,
To there assail the pilgrim in his pass,
Bash out his brains, usurp his anguish-garnered hoard?

Fear! Fear! Midstream the exile wavers,
Tortured by guilt, doubt-wrung, his guts all gone.
About his loins the death-dragged water seethes,
Creeling his doom, and the grainy flints of fate
Sift and suck out beneath his terror-fastened feet.

No help. No hope. Nothing. If this be Esau
Then Jacob meets his star. Brother to brother,
Shadow to lipless shadow, the twin identities
Confront. Deep down his spirit gropes. Desperate
He grapples that stranger in one fierce convulsive rush.

This, then, at last, the divine engagement.
Who wrestled with his brother in the womb
Wrestles now the angel. The years go down tumultuous
Beneath his trampling feet. O mother-favored son
What deed of truth did all those phantasies prefix?

One queasy crime—and the score-long exiled years!
How many mockeries of the inscrutable archetypes
Must we endure to meet our integration?
Is it fate or merely malice that has made
Us overreach our brother in the burdened womb?

Is it fate or merely malice that entraps
Us early in our own self-hugging hearts,
Darlings of our mother's doting eye, to steal
The kindly blinded father's foremost blessing,
Too soon seize up the giddy promises of God.

Fatality or malice, either-or, that curse
Curses us cold. We in our sin will never see
The glad, long-looked-for land. Mother-duped exiles,
Skewered on our father's guilt, we learn, we learn
Too late to face the angel, engage the hidden God.

All night they fought. All night the home-starved son
Turned in torment in the angel's withering grasp,
There on the trampled weeds by the root-grown shore
Where the sullen winter freshet, flushed with grit,
Rushed by like passion in the black prophetic night.

What vast eternities hang here contained?
What conflicts down the long genetic line
Suffer their extirpation in the wrestler's stance?
High overhead the great globed constellations
Hover like circling birds above the struggled heads.

And far down the planet's dark nocturnal side
The night-wombed nations murmur into birth.
His sistered wives, confused and terrified,
Twin aspects of his dark divided life,
Crouch in the weltering night and moan for his reprieve.

Dogged the man fights on, grappled wrist and knee,
And when the dawn blurs in the time-pressed angel
Glances at the east and makes to go.
But the exile, obdurate, closed in the unremitting
Grasp, exacts the specific blessing that he needs.

The man has won. Standing at last alone
He staggers on the twisted thew, if not
Invincible at least undaunted. This anguish
In the sinew is his sign, his final liberation,
Seal of the smiling God, the serene benediction.

Hurt but truly healed he sways, who seized
In the heart's black hole the angel of intellection,
And rose renewed, in the soul's great upsurge shaped.
His painful deprivations all converge
To make the anguished synthesis of his perfection.

And is called Israel, striver with God, and limps
Into the light of the huge ingesting sun, and meets

The long-feared brother: who beholds a saint,
Measured in the furious siege of grace, and seeing
Weeps on that placid neck, kisses the God-calmed face.

Brother Antoninus

50.   HOW SAMSON BORE AWAY
THE GATES OF GAZA

A Negro Sermon

Once, in a night as black as ink,
She drove him out when he would not drink.
Round the house there were men in wait
Asleep in rows by the Gaza gate.
But the Holy Spirit was in this man.
Like a gentle wind he crept and ran.
("It is midnight," said the big town clock.)

He lifted the gates up, post and lock.
The hole in the wall was high and wide
When he bore away old Gaza's pride
Into the deep of the night:—
The bold Jack Johnson Israelite,—
Samson—
The Judge,
The Nazarite.

The air was black, like the smoke of a dragon.
Samson's heart was as big as a wagon.
He sang like a shining golden fountain.
He sweated up to the top of the mountain.
He threw down the gates with a noise like judgment.
And the quails all ran with the big arousement.

But he wept—"I must not love tough queens,
And spend on them my hard earned means.
I told that girl I would drink no more.

Therefore she drove me from her door.
Oh sorrow!
Sorrow!
I cannot hide.
Oh Lord look down from your chariot side.
You made me Judge, and I am not wise.
I am weak as a sheep for all my size."

Let Samson
Be coming
Into your mind.

The moon shone out, the stars were gay.
He saw the foxes run and play.
He rent his garments, he rolled around
In deep repentance on the ground.

Then he felt a honey in his soul.
Grace abounding made him whole.
Then he saw the Lord in a chariot blue.
The gorgeous stallions whinnied and flew.
The iron wheels hummed an old hymn-tune
And crunched in thunder over the moon.
And Samson shouted to the sky:
"My Lord, my Lord is riding high."

Like a steed, he pawed the gates with his hoof.
He rattled the gates like rocks on the roof,
And danced in the night
On the mountain-top,
Danced in the deep of the night:
The Judge, the holy Nazarite,
Whom ropes and chains could never bind.

Let Samson
Be coming
Into your mind.

Whirling his arms, like a top he sped.
His long black hair flew round his head
Like an outstretched net of silky cord,
Like a wheel of the chariot of the Lord.

Let Samson
Be coming
Into your mind.

Samson saw the sun anew.
He left the gates in the grass and dew.
He went to a county-seat a-nigh
Found a harlot proud and high:
Philistine that no man could tame—
Delilah was her lady-name.
Oh sorrow,
Sorrow,
She was too wise.
She cut off his hair,
She put out his eyes.

Let Samson
Be coming
Into your mind.

Vachel Lindsay

51.　THE ELEVENTH COMMANDMENT

I

When Moses came down from the mountain and the cloud,
He came alone down the rocks and there alone a while,
The air above him empty and all still, he stood.
There had been trumpets in the fire, but he was whole.
He was Moses, older than old, remembering what he saw,
Saying to himself, a white light in his face,
What he must say to the people, remembering the law.

A man can live to an age that is outside age,
Where forgetting is forgotten, and remembering
Is the hand's motion turning an earlier page.
Nothing is unimportant there, and everything
Is written on one page or another of the book.
Whatever the old men need to know, they know
They have but to turn the pages, turn, and look.

Moses would say everything God had said to him
To the people waiting in the valley below to hear,
The cubits of the tabernacle he would build for them,
The cornering, the colors. But there was one more
Commandment than ten. Only an auditor
Very old, an old man with Moses' many years,
Could know after the ten commandments one more.

He had been up there a long time hearing what he heard.
He had carried up there all he had ever known.
Now he must utter before and after God's word
What both knew. And shining, Moses went down.
He read from the tablet the last word: Listen.
Those who were to be the new world heard the law,
And Moses began again, with the first word: Listen.

IV

It is not enough that one's own inner voice
Make of one's life a lifelong monotone.
I, me, mine, to-for-because-of me, rejoice
A man but little, then less, less, and none.
What does he hear for news who has only heard
From his own island? It is a treasure of dust
On the wind when he unlocks his word-hoard.

Moses' commandment opens the world's mouth
To utter the memory of life. One listener
Is man multiplied, man taking in time's breath

To be in one body ancestor and heir.
He owes one duty thus: Attention. Man
If he means to live shall hold his whole mind
At ready awake. With this the law began.
So Moses brought the eleventh commandment down,
Knowing his will stir, his blood hasten
That the word be said aloud, the word be known,
That on it all men might take hold and fasten
On it, and hear it in all tongues: Listen.
He lifted the tablets up before them saying
The word that gave them all words: Listen.

John Holmes
From *The Eleventh Commandment*
Phi Beta Kappa Poem, Harvard University, 1956

52.   MALACHI

Grim messenger of God,
Nameless down aeons of forgotten years,
He thought it enough to write his name
In the Father's Book of Remembrance.

Others saw the shadow;
He groped for the light,
And found it.
"God has forgotten," they said,
"The people of His love."
He answered: "God remembers;
"He will return
"To those who return to Him."
Cynics mocked him:
"God knows and yet we suffer?
"Your God is a weakling
"Or, possibly, afraid."
(His God a weakling?)
"No," he thundered.

"God's flaming day is near;
"It is darkened in dawning
"By man's unrighteousness.
"I will send my messenger,
"Saith the Lord of Hosts;
"And who may abide his coming?
"Who shall stand when he appears?
"For he is like a forger's fire
"Or a fuller's acid."

He saw the sins of his friends
And denounced them fearlessly:
"Every man dealt treacherously with his brother,"
And priests, in the name of God,
Called mummery religion.
He saw its hollowness.
"The heathen," he sighed
"Serve God more truly
"Than the children of His choice."

Foredreaming the faith of the future,
He knew and preached the truth:
One honors his Father
When he loves and serves his brother:
"Have not all of us one Father?"

His was the shining vision,
The task of the pioneer:
He blazed the trail of a Brother
Who fared beyond the sun
And fathomed its mystery:
"I am the light of the world.
"God is a spirit,
"And they that worship Him
"Must worship Him in spirit
"And in truth."

Earl Marlatt

53. ZECHARIAH

Among a people who doubted
That a better dawn would break,
One believed,
Through the after-dusk of war,
In a God of mercy and peace.

He saw the flash of light,
Or wings, against the steel-blue dark.
"Angels," he said,
"In the glen of the myrtle trees". . . .
Adventurers from God,
Craftsmen for God,
Eager to build His city
And crown it with a Temple:
Priests and kings, obedient to the Voice:
"Not by might, nor by power,
"But by my spirit,
"Saith the Lord of Hosts."

He saw the Adversary humbled
And banished to the vale of weeping.
He saw the Holy City,
Peopled with patriarchs
And women mothering sturdy children.

On a new Sinai
He heard a new Law for all nations:
"Execute true judgment;
"Show mercy and compassion
"Every man to his brother;
"Oppress not the widow,
"Nor the fatherless,
"The stranger, nor the poor;
"Let none imagine in his heart
"Suspicion of his neighbor."

He brought the balm of peace
To a world wounded by war.
Comrades said of him:
"We will go with you;
"For we have heard
"That the Lord, our God, is with you."

Earl Marlatt

54.   JONAH

As I lie here in the sun
And gaze out, a day's journey, over Nineveh,
The sailors in the dark hold cry to me:
"What meanest thou, O sleeper? Arise and call upon
Thy God; pray with us, that we perish not."

All thy billows and thy waves passed over me.
The waters compassed me, the weeds were wrapped about my head;
The earth with her bars was about me forever.
A naked worm, a man no longer,
I writhed beneath the dead:

But thou art merciful.
When my soul was dead within me I remembered thee,
From the depths I cried to thee. For thou art merciful:
Thou hast brought my life up from corruption,
O Lord my God. . . . When the king said, "Who can tell

But God may yet repent, and turn away
From his fierce anger, that we perish not?"
My heart fell; for I knew his grace of old—
In my own country, Lord, did I not say
That thou art merciful?

Now take, Lord, I beseech thee,
My life from me; it is better that I die . . .

But I hear, "Dost thou well, then, to be angry?"
And I say nothing, and look bitterly
Across the city; a young gourd grows over me

And shades me—and I slumber, clean of grief.
I was glad of the gourd. But God prepared
A worm that gnawed the gourd; but God prepared
The east wind, the sun beat upon my head
Till I cried, "Let me die!" And God said, "Doest thou well

To be angry for the gourd?"
And I said in my anger, "I do well
To be angry, even unto death." But the Lord God
Said to me, "Thou hast had pity on the gourd"—
And I wept, to hear its dead leaves rattle—

"Which came up in a night, and perished in a night.
And should I not spare Nineveh, that city
Wherein are more than six-score thousand persons
Who cannot tell their left hand from their right;
And also much cattle?"

Randall Jarrell

55.   BELSHAZZAR

Belshazzar had a letter,—
He never had but one;
Belshazzar's correspondent
Concluded and begun
In that immortal copy
The conscience of us all
Can read without its glasses
On revelation's wall.

Emily Dickinson

56. WEEPING AND SINGING

"They that sow in tears shall reap in joy."

From a land of milk and honey,
From hills and rivers clear,
the people of Israel went forth,
weeping.

Pillars of fire and cloud
went on before their steps
and Israel crossed the desert,
weeping.

The captives lifted up their
cities of mighty walls
and they gave thanks to God,
weeping.

Their lances became harrows,
their swords were turned into ploughs,
night and day they laboured,
weeping.

The sea of fiery waters
they crossed over with their horses,
the tempest fell upon them,
weeping.

They were walled about
in the shadow of the ghettos
but they found out the light,
weeping.

The Sabbath was their buckler,
their isle, their candelabrum,

and they called the Sabbath holy,
weeping.

Taunted and spat upon,
bent low above the earth,
they sow without hate or rest,
weeping.

Tomorrow the sun will smile
upon the seed-rich fields
and then, then we shall reap,
singing, brothers, singing.

Cesar Tiempo
tr. *from the Spanish by Donald Devenish Walsh*

57.   SAINT JOHN

A wild pleasure for Saint John
In the desert wandering,
Under red cliffs pondering,
Shaggy-headed facing dawn,
Leaning by lost pools to drink
Meditating at their brink,
Eating fruit of locust trees,
Stealing honey from the small fierce bees.

A wild pleasure for Saint John
Tawny as the beasts, and thin,
Wrapped about by a goat's skin
(Nothing made by man or woman)
Hairy hide on hairy breast,
Curled in a beast's cave to rest,
Dreaming with a saint's elation
Of the terrible and glorious pathway to salvation.

A wild pleasure for Saint John
In a burning recognition

To have known his Lord and mission,
From his desert to have gone
Shrilling great outrageous things
In the angry ears of kings,
Till that head from desert sands,
A princess, hot with dancing, carried between her hands.

Elizabeth J. Coatsworth

58.   PETER AND JOHN

Twelve good friends
Walked under the leaves,
Binding the ends
Of the barley sheaves.

Peter and John
Lay down to sleep
Pillowed upon
A haymaker's heap.

John and Peter
Lay down to dream.
The air was sweeter
'Than honey and cream.

Peter was bred
In the salty cold:
His hair was red
And his eyes were gold.

John had a mouth
Like a wing bent down:
His brow was smooth
And his eyes were brown.

Peter to slumber
Sank like a stone,

Of all their number
The bravest one.

John more slowly
Composed himself,
Young and holy
Among the twelve.

John as he slept
Cried out in grief,
Turned and wept
On the golden leaf:

"Peter, Peter,
Stretch me your hand
Across the glitter
Of the harvest land!

"Peter, Peter,
Give me a sign!
This was a bitter
Dream of mine—

"Bitter as aloes
It parched my tongue.
Upon the gallows
My life was hung.

"Sharp it seemed
As a bloody sword.
Peter, I dreamed
I was Christ the Lord!"

Peter turned
To holy Saint John:
His body burned
In the falling sun.

In the falling sun
He burned like flame:
"John, Saint John,
I have dreamed the same!

"My bones were hung
On an elder tree;
Bells were rung
Over Galilee.

"A silver penny
Sealed each of my eyes.
Many and many
A cock crew thrice."

When Peter's word
Was spoken and done,
"Were you Christ the Lord
In your dream?" said John.

"No," said the other,
"That I was not.
I was our brother
Iscariot."

Elinor Wylie

59. MAGDALENE

I

As soon as night comes my demon springs up out of the ground.
This is the price I pay for my past.
They come, those memories of vice,
And fall to gnawing at my heart.
Those memories of days when I, a slave
To the whims and quirks of males,
Was but a demoniac fool and the street was all my shelter.

A few scant moments still remain
And then a silence as of the grave will fall.
But before they pass I, having reached
The very limit of my life,
Am shattering that life at Thy feet
As if it were an alabaster vessel.

Oh, where would I now be,
My Master and my Saviour,
If eternity were not awaiting me
Of nights, standing by my bed
Like a new visitor enticed
Into the net of my profession?

But still, I would have Thee expound for me the meaning
Of sin, and death, and hell and brimstone fire—
When I, before the eyes of all, have grown into one
With Thee, even as scion and tree,
Because my yearning is beyond all measure.

When, Jesus, I embrace Thy feet
As I support them on my knees
It may be that I am learning to embrace
The squared beam of the Cross
And, bereft of my senses, am straining for Thy body
As I prepare Thee for Thy interment.

II

People are tidying up before the holiday.
Aloof from all this bustle,
I am anointing Thy most immaculate feet
With myrrh from a small bowl.

I grope for and cannot find Thy sandals.
I can see naught because of my tears.
Strands of my loosened hair have fallen
Like a pall over my eyes.

I have set Thy feet upon my lap,
I have poured my tears over them, Jesus;
I have entwined them with the string of beads from around my neck,
I have buried them in my hair, as in the folds of a burnous.

I see the future in such detail
As if Thou hast made it stand still.
At this moment I can foretell events
With the fatidical clairvoyance of the Sybils.

The veil will fall on the morrow within the Temple.
We will be huddled in a knot off to one side.
And the earth will rock underfoot—
Out of pity for me, perhaps.

The ranks of the guard will realign
And the mounted soldiers will start dispersing.
Just as a waterspout in a storm strains upward
So will that Cross be straining to reach the sky.

I shall prostrate myself on the earth at the foot of the crucifix.
I shall make my heart stop its beating, I shall bite my lips.
Thou hast spread Thy arms to embrace far too many,
Flinging Thy hands out till they reach the ends of the crossbeam.

For whom in this world is all this breadth,
So much agony and such power?
Are there so many souls and lives in this universe—
So many settlements, and rivers and groves?

Yet three days such as this shall pass
And they shall thrust me into such a void
That during this brief interval of time
I shall, even before the Resurrection, attain my full stature.

Boris Pasternak
tr. from the Russian by Bernard Guilbert Guerney

60.   IN THE SERVANTS' QUARTERS

"Man, you too, aren't you, one of these rough followers of the
                                                    criminal?
All hanging hereabout to gather how he's going to bear
Examination in the hall." She flung disdainful glances on
The shabby figure standing at the fire with others there,
   Who warmed them by its flare.

"No indeed, my skipping maiden: I know nothing of the trial here,
Or criminal, if so he be.—I chanced to come this way,
And the fire shone out into the dawn, and morning airs are cold now;
I, too, was drawn in part by charms I see before me play,
   That I see not every day."

"Ha, ha!" then laughed the constables who also stood to warm
                                                    themselves,
The while another maiden scrutinized his features hard,
As the blaze threw into contrast every line and knot that wrinkled
                                                    them,
Exclaiming, "Why, last night when he was brought in by the guard,
   You were with him in the yard!"

"Nay, nay, you teasing wench, I say! You know you speak mistakenly,
Cannot a tired pedestrian who has legged it long and far
Here on his way from northern parts, engrossed in humble marketings,
Come in and rest awhile, although judicial doings are
   Afoot by morning star?"

"O, come, come!" laughed the constables. "Why, man, you speak the
                                                    dialect
He uses in his answers; you can hear him up the stairs.
So own it. We sha'n't hurt ye. There he's speaking now! His syllables
Are those you sound yourself when you are talking unawares,
   As the pretty girl declares."

"And you shudder when his chain clinks!" she rejoined. "O yes, I
                                                    noticed it.

And you winced, too, when those cuffs they gave him echoed to us
                                                            here.
They'll soon be coming down, and you may then have to defend
                                                         yourself
Unless you hold your tongue, or go away and keep you clear
    When he's led to judgment near!"

"No, I'll be damned in hell if I know anything about the man!
No single thing about him more than everybody knows.
Must not I even warm my hands but I am charged with
                                    blasphemies?" . . .
—His face convulses as the morning cock that moment crows,
    And he droops, and turns, and goes.

Thomas Hardy

61.   PETER

Lifted by the teaching of a Master
From the pallid shores of a lake
To the azure heights it mirrored,
He fell before a woman's scorn;
Three times he denied his Lord;
And immediately the cock crew.

He was crucified head-downward
Because he thought himself unworthy
To die the death of Jesus.

Denial,
Cock-crow,
Crucifixion—
His was a sacred way
That only the strong dare follow.

Earl Marlatt

62. STARLIGHT LIKE INTUITION
PIERCED THE TWELVE

The starlight's intuition pierced the twelve,
The brittle night sky sparkled like a tune
Tinkled and tapped out on the xylophone.
Empty and vain, a glittering dune, the moon
Arose too big, and, in the mood which ruled,
Seemed like a useless beauty in a pit;
And then one said, after he carefully spat:
"No matter what we do, he looks at it!

"I cannot see a child or find a girl
Beyond his smile which glows like that spring moon."
"—Nothing no more the same," the second said,
"Though all may be forgiven, never quite healed
The wound I bear as witness, standing by;
No ceremony surely appropriate,
Nor secret love, escape or sleep because
No matter what I do, he looks at it—"

"Now," said the third, "no thing will be the same:
I am as one who never shuts his eyes,
The sea and sky no more are marvellous,
And I no longer understand surprise!"
"Now," said the fourth, "nothing will be enough
—I heard his voice accomplishing all wit:
No word can be unsaid, no deed withdrawn
—No matter what is said, he measures it!"

"Vision, imagination, hope or dream,
Believed, denied, the scene we wished to see?
It does not matter in the least: for what
Is altered, if it is not true? That we
Saw goodness, as it is—*this* is the awe
And the abyss which we will not forget,
His story now the sky which holds all thought:
No matter what I think, I think of it!"

"And I will never be what once I was,"
Said one for long as narrow as a knife,
"And we will never be what once we were;
We have died once; this is a second life."
"My mind is spilled in moral chaos," one
Righteous as Job exclaimed, "now infinite
Suspicion of my heart stems what I will
—No matter what I choose, he stares at it!"

"I am as one native in summer places
—Ten weeks' excitement paid for by the rich;
Debauched by that and then all winter bored,"
The sixth declared. "His peak left us a ditch!"
"He came to make this life more difficult,"
The seventh said, "No one will ever fit
His measure's heights, all is inadequate:
No matter what I do, what good is it?"

"He gave forgiveness to us: what a gift!"
The eighth chimed in. "But now we know how much
Must be forgiven. But if forgiven, what?
The crime which was will be; and the least touch
Revives the memory: what is forgiveness worth?"
The ninth spoke thus: "Who now will ever sit
At ease in Zion at the Easter feast?
No matter what the place, he touches it!"

"And I will always stammer, since he spoke,"
One, who had been most eloquent, said, stammering.
"I looked too long at the sun; like too much light,
So too much goodness is a boomerang,"
Laughed the eleventh of the troop. "I must
Try what he tried: I saw the infinite
Who walked the lake and raised the hopeless dead:
No matter what the feat, he first accomplished it!"

So spoke the twelfth; and then the twelve in chorus:
"Unspeakable unnatural goodness is

Risen and shines, and never will ignore us;
He glows forever in all consciousness;
Forgiveness, love, and hope possess the pit,
And bring our endless guilt, like shadow's bars:
No matter what we do, he stares at it!
What pity then deny? what debt defer?
We know he looks at us like all the stars,
And we shall never be as once we were,
This life will never be what once it was!"

Delmore Schwartz

V nativity

"The stars shall bend their voices,
And every stone shall cry"

63.   ADVENT MEDITATION

Rorate Coeli desuper, et nubes pluant Justum.
Aperiatur Terra, et germinet Salvatorem.

No sudden thing of glory and fear
Was the Lord's coming; but the dear
   Slow Nature's days followed each other
   To form the Saviour from His Mother
—One of the children of the year.

The earth, the rain, received the trust,
—The sun and dews, to frame the Just.
   He drew His daily life from these,
   According to His own decrees
Who makes man from the fertile dust.

Sweet summer and the winter wild,
These brought Him forth, the Undefiled.
   The happy Springs renewed again
   His daily bread, the growing grain.
The food and raiment of the Child.

                              Alice Meynell

64.   BIRTH OF MARY

O what must it have cost the angels
not suddenly to burst into song, as one bursts into tears,
since indeed they knew: on this night the mother is being
born to the boy, the One, who shall soon appear.

Soaring they held themselves silent and showed the direction
where, alone, Joachim's farm lay;
ah, they felt in themselves and in space the pure precipitation,
but none might go down to him.

For the two were already quite beside themselves with ado.
A neighbor-woman came and played wise and did not know how,

and the old man, carefully, went and withheld the mooing
Of a dark cow. For so it had never yet been.

Rainer Maria Rilke
tr. *from the German by M. D. Herter Norton*

65.   JOSEPH'S SUSPICION

And the angel spoke and made an effort
with the man, who clenched his fists;
But dost thou not see by every fold
that she is cool as God's early day?

Yet the other looked somberly at him,
murmuring only: What has changed her so?
But at that the angel cried: Carpenter,
dost thou not yet see that the Lord God is acting?

Because thou makest boards, in thy pride,
wouldst thou really call him to account
who modestly out of the same wood
makes leaves burgeon and buds swell?

He understood. And as he now raised his eyes
very frightened, to the angel,
he was gone. He pushed his heavy
cap slowly off. Then he sang praise.

Rainer Maria Rilke
tr. *from the German by M. D. Herter Norton*

66.   A CHRISTMAS HYMN

And some of the Pharisees from among the multitude said unto
him, Master, rebuke thy disciples.
And he answered and said unto them, I tell you that, if these
should hold their peace, the stones would immediately cry out.

St. Luke XIX, 39–40

A stable-lamp is lighted
Whose glow shall wake the sky;
The stars shall bend their voices,
And every stone shall cry.
And every stone shall cry,
And straw like gold shall shine;
A barn shall harbor heaven,
A stall become a shrine.

This child through David's city
Shall ride in triumph by;
The palm shall strew its branches,
And every stone shall cry.
And every stone shall cry,
Though heavy, dull, and dumb,
And lie within the roadway
To pave his kingdom come.

Yet he shall be forsaken,
And yielded up to die;
The sky shall groan and darken,
And every stone shall cry.
And every stone shall cry
For stony hearts of men:
God's blood upon the spearhead,
God's love refused again.

But now, as at the ending,
The low is lifted high;
The stars shall bend their voices,
And every stone shall cry.
And every stone shall cry
In praises of the child
By whose descent among us
The worlds are reconciled.

                              Richard Wilbur

67.   SPECIAL STARLIGHT

The Creator of night and of birth
was the Maker of the stars.
Shall we look up now at stars in Winter
And call them always sweeter friends
Because this story of a Mother and a Child
Never is told with the stars left out?

Is it a Holy Night now when a child issues
Out of the dark and the unknown
Into the starlight?

Down a Winter evening sky
when a woman hovers
between two great doorways,
between entry and exit,
between pain to be laughed at,
joy to be wept over—
do the silver-white lines
then come from holy stars?
shall the Newcomer, the Newborn,
be given soft flannels,
swaddling-cloths called Holy?

Shall all wanderers over the earth, all homeless ones,
All against whom doors are shut and words spoken—

Shall these find the earth less strange tonight?
Shall they hear news, a whisper on the night wind?
"A Child is born." "The meek shall inherit the earth."
"And they crucified Him . . . they spat upon Him.
And He rose from the dead."

Shall a quiet dome of stars high over
Make signs and a friendly language
Among all the nations?

Shall they yet gather with no clenched fists at all,
And look into each other's faces and see eye to eye,
And find ever new testaments of man as a sojourner
And a toiler and a brother of fresh understandings?

> Shall there be now always
> believers and more believers
> of sunset and moonrise,
> of moonset and dawn,
> of wheeling numbers of stars,
> and wheels within wheels?

Shall plain habitations off the well-known roads
Count now for a little more than they used to?

Shall plain ways and people held close to earth
be reckoned among things to be written about?

Shall tumult, grandeur, fanfare, panoply, prepared loud noises
Stand equal to a quiet heart, thoughts, vast dreams
Of men conquering the earth by conquering themselves?
Is there a time for ancient genius of man
To be set for comparison with the latest generations?
Is there a time for stripping to simple, childish questions?

> On a Holy Night we may say:
> The Creator of night and of birth
> was the Maker of the stars.
>
> *Carl Sandburg*

68.   UNTO US A SON IS GIVEN

> Given, not lent,
> And not withdrawn—once sent,
> This Infant of mankind, this One,
> Is still the little welcome Son.

New every year,
New born and newly dear,
He comes with tidings and a song,
The ages long, the ages long;

Even as the cold
Keen winter grows not old
As childhood is so fresh, foreseen,
And spring in the familiar green.

Sudden as sweet
Come the expected feet.
All joy is young, and new all art,
And He, too, Whom we have by heart.

                                        Alice Meynell

69.   BIRTH OF CHRIST

Hadst thou not simplicity, how should
that happen to thee which now lights up the night?
See, the God who rumbled over nations
makes himself mild and in thee comes into the world.

Hadst thou imagined him greater?

What is greatness? Right through all measures
that he crosses goes his straight destiny.
Even a star has no such path,
see thou, these kings are great,

and they drag before thy lap

treasures that they hold to be the greatest,
and thou art perhaps astonished at this gift—:
but look into the folds of thy shawl,
how even now he has exceeded all.

All amber that one ships afar,
all ornament of gold and the aromatic spice
that spreads blurringly in the senses:
all this was of rapid brevity,
and who knows but one has regretted it.

But (thou wilt see): He brings joy.

Rainer Maria Rilke
tr. *from the German by M. D. Herter Norton*

70.   MANGERS

Who knows the name and country now,
    Of that rich man who lived of old;
Whose horses fed at silver mangers,
    And drank of wine from troughs of gold?

He who was in a manger born,
    By gold and silver undefiled—
Is known as Christ to every man,
    And Jesus to a little child.

W. H. Davies

71.   ON CHRISTMAS EVE

On Christmas Eve the ox, the ass, the sheep
Spoke to the Christ-child as he lay asleep.

Said the ass:
"You will carry heavy burdens, little Brother.
Mighty loads will be put upon you, little Brother."

Said the sheep:
"They will shear you of your fleece, little Brother.
They will strip you on a cold day, little Brother."

Said the ox:
"You will draw a plow through stony soil, little Brother.
Wood shall be laid across your neck, little Brother."

So softly spoke the ox, the ass, the sheep;
They troubled not the little Jesus' sleep . . .

Edith Lovejoy Pierce

72.   THE   GIFT

As the wise men of old brought gifts
    guided by a star
        to the humble birthplace

of the god of love,
    the devils
        as an old print shows
retreated in confusion.

    What could a baby know
        of gold ornaments
or frankincense and myrrh,
    of priestly robes
        and devout genuflections?

But the imagination
    knows all stories
        before they are told
and knows the truth of this one
    past all defection

The rich gifts
    so unsuitable for a child
        though devoutly proffered,
stood for all that love can bring.
    The men were old
        how could they know

of a mother's needs
  or a child's
    appetite?

But as they kneeled
  the child was fed.
    They saw it
and gave praise!
    A miracle

had taken place,
  hard gold to love,
a mother's milk!
  before
    their wondering eyes.

The ass brayed
  the cattle lowed.
    It was their nature.

All men by their nature give praise.
  It is all
    they can do.

The very devils
  by their flight give praise.
    What is death,
beside this?
  Nothing. The wise men
    came with gift

and bowed down
  to worship
    this perfection.

                    William Carlos Williams

73.   JOURNEY OF THE MAGI

'A cold coming we had of it,
Just the worst time of the year
For a journey, and such a long journey:
The ways deep and the weather sharp,
The very dead of winter.'
And the camels galled, sore-footed, refractory,
Lying down in the melting snow.
There were times we regretted
The summer palaces on slopes, the terraces,
And the silken girls bringing sherbet.
Then the camel men cursing and grumbling
And running away, and wanting their liquor and women,
And the night-fires going out, and the lack of shelters,
And the cities hostile and the towns unfriendly
And the villages dirty and charging high prices:
A hard time we had of it.
At the end we preferred to travel all night,
Sleeping in snatches,
With the voices singing in our ears, saying
That this was all folly.

Then at dawn we came to a temperate valley,
Wet, below the snow line, smelling of vegetation;
With a running stream and a water-mill beating the darkness,
And three trees on the low sky,
And an old horse galloped away in the meadow.
Then we came to a tavern with vine-leaves over the lintel,
Six hands at an open door dicing for pieces of silver,
And feet kicking the empty wine-skins.
But there was no information, and so we continued
And arrived at evening, not a moment too soon
Finding the place; it was (you may say) satisfactory.

All this was a long time ago, I remember,
And I would do it again, but set down

This set down
This: were we led all that way for
Birth or Death? There was a Birth, certainly,
We had evidence and no doubt. I had seen birth and death,
But had thought they were different; the Birth was
Hard and bitter agony for us, like Death, our death.
We returned to our places, these Kingdoms,
But no longer at ease here, in the old dispensation,
With an alien people clutching their gods.
I should be glad of another death.

T. S. Eliot

74.   A CHRISTMAS CAROL

Star that shone on Bethlehem, shine on London city.
    Shine upon the pathway of each stumbling wayfarer.
Shine upon the crowds, and back to light, O star of pity,
    Guide them with their sacrifice of frankincense and myrrh.

Guide them, loved and loveless, wise and foolish, high and lowly.
    They are seeking all a kingdom, but they have all gone astray.
Guide them through the mist, and, with their shoes besmeared yet
                                                            holy,
    Set their faltering footsteps once again upon the way.

Some of them are blinded by the rich man's garish table,
    And some of them by envy that the table is not theirs.
Guide them back, ah guide them, to the cold and empty stable;
    Guide them to the manger where the oxen eat the tares.

All of them seek succour from a food that cannot feed them;
    All of them are lost because they strive to understand.
Tell them, star of Noel, that a little child shall lead them
    Back into the Kingdom through the gates of wonderland.

Star that shone on Bethlehem, shine on London city.
    Shine upon the pathway of each stumbling wayfarer.

Shine upon the crowds, and back to light, O star of pity,
   Guide them with their sacrifice of frankincense and myrrh.

                                        Gilbert Thomas

75. THE OXEN

Christmas Eve, and twelve of the clock.
   "Now they are all on their knees,"
An elder said as we sat in a flock
   By the embers in hearthside ease.

We pictured the meek mild creatures where
   They dwelt in their strawy pen,
Nor did it occur to one of us there
   To doubt they were kneeling then.

So fair a fancy few would weave
   In these years! Yet, I feel,
If someone said on Christmas Eve,
   "Come; see the oxen kneel,

"In the lonely barton by yonder coomb
   Our childhood used to know,"
I should go with him in the gloom,
   Hoping it might be so.

                                        Thomas Hardy

76. THE HOUSE OF CHRISTMAS

There fared a mother driven forth
Out of an inn to roam;
In the place where she was homeless
All men are at home.
The crazy stable close at hand,
With shaking timber and shifting sand,
Grew a stronger thing to abide and stand
Than the square stones of Rome.

For men are homesick in their homes,
And strangers under the sun,
And they lay their heads in a foreign land
Whenever the day is done.
Here we have battle and blazing eyes,
And chance and honour and high surprise,
But our homes are under miraculous skies
Where the yule tale was begun.

A Child in a foul stable,
Where the beasts feed and foam;
Only where He was homeless
Are you and I at home;
We have hands that fashion and heads that know,
But our hearts we lost—how long ago!
In a place no chart nor ship can show
Under the sky's dome.

This world is wild as an old wives' tale,
And strange the plain things are,
The earth is enough and the air is enough
For our wonder and our war;
But our rest is as far as the fire-drake swings
And our peace is put in impossible things
Where clashed and thundered unthinkable wings
Round an incredible star.

To an open house in the evening
Home shall men come,
To an older place than Eden
And a taller town than Rome.
To the end of the way of the wandering star,
To the things that cannot be and that are,
To the place where God was homeless
And all men are at home.

　　　　　　　　　　　　　　G. K. Chesterton

77. CHRIST CLIMBED DOWN

Christ climbed down
from His bare Tree
this year
and ran away to where
there were no rootless Christmas trees
hung with candycanes and breakable stars

Christ climbed down
from His bare Tree
this year
and ran away to where
there were no gilded Christmas trees
and no tinsel Christmas trees
and no tinfoil Chrismas trees
and no pink plastic Christmas trees
and no gold Christmas trees
and no powderblue Christmas trees
hung with electric candles
and encircled by tin electric trains
and clever cornball relatives

Christ climbed down
from His bare Tree
this year
and ran away to where
no intrepid Bible salesmen
covered the territory
in two-tone cadillacs
and where no Sears Roebuck crèches
complete with plastic babe in manger
arrived by parcel post
the babe by special delivery
and where no televised Wise Men
praised the Lord Calvert Whiskey

Christ climbed down
from His bare Tree
this year
and ran away to where
no fat handshaking stranger
in a red flannel suit
and a fake white beard
went around passing himself off
as some sort of North Pole saint
crossing the desert to Bethlehem
Pennsylvania
in a Volkswagon sled
drawn by rollicking Adirondack reindeer
with German names
and bearing sacks of Humble Gifts
from Saks Fifth Avenue
for everybody's imagined Christ child

Christ climbed down
from His bare Tree
this year
and ran away to where
no Bing Crosby carollers
groaned of a tight Christmas
and where no Radio City angels
iceskated wingless
thru a winter wonderland
into a jinglebell heaven
daily at 8:30
with Midnight Mass matinees

Christ climbed down
from His bare Tree
this year
and softly stole away into
some anonymous Mary's womb again
where in the darkest night

of everybody's anonymous soul
He awaits again
an unimaginable
and impossibly
Immaculate Reconception
the very craziest
of Second Comings

Lawrence Ferlinghetti

78.   THE LIGHT IN THE TEMPLE

Into the temple the gaunt old saint strode, by the Spirit led.
There a man, and a woman, and a small child sacrificed.
There, between seven-branched candlesticks, two dead wood-pigeons
bled;
But Simeon saw the Christ.

For the child turned on Simeon that dark gaze that charms and
alarms,
And Israel's soul was stricken with a pang like the pain of the sword,
And Simeon's spirit quickened, and he lifted the child in his arms;
He lifted up Christ the Lord.

Hoarsely he cried, "O now Thou lettest thy servant depart in peace.
I have walked through dragon fires of darkness wherein thy world is
snared;
Yet, before the face of all, this hour, I have seen what doth not cease:
In the child, salvation prepared;

A light to lighten the Gentiles; Thine own people Israel's glory!"
. . . Nearly two thousand years ago were those words by the prophet
said.
Now, in the day of apocalypse, we ponder the troubled story.
Our heaven quakes overhead.

Simeon blessed them, and said unto Mary the mother, "Behold this
child.

He is set for the fall and rising again of many in Israel.
And a sword shall pierce through thine own heart, from him, the
                                        small and mild—
    And the heart of Mankind as well."

Dark with famine lies half the world; in the core of life is danger;
With expectation the people cry and clamor on every hand.
And even once more, through blowing snow, there comes to Mankind
                                        a stranger;
    The Stranger, through every land.

For a moment stand with the prophet then, when the simple truth
                                        was graved
Deep in his soul; when mightier wings no chaos can destroy
Lightened on high; and there came to men, in the ancient city of
                                        David,
    Good tidings of great joy.
                                        William Rose Benét

VI   holy week, easter

"I shall descend into my grave,
And on the third day rise again"

79.   THE WORDS OF JESUS

When you read what he said
It never stays on the page,
It comes alive in the air. Aramaic or Greek
I have not, but the words glow and speak
Even in English, the words have joy like rage,
They step over aeons, march over ages,
They are not antlike marks on whispering pages!

How was the phrase first cast? I do not know.
Can we trust Matthew or Mark or Luke or John,
Paul to Timothy, Titus or Philemon—
The other Epistles—or Peter, or James, or Jude?
How should the Hebrew go?
How should, for instance, this parable be construed?
I do not know. I only charge you, look—
The words live! They rise right out of the book!

They whirl in a column of light, a shaft of wonder.
They shatteringly amaze, and almost frighten.
You momentarily expect them to lighten
And thunder. . . .
And then, they are limpid sky, green hills, still rivers
Of silvery Galilee, where not a tendril quivers.
Clear and clean and sane—till you could almost forget
The dark, the horrible pain, the anguish, the bloody sweat. . . .

William Rose Benét

80.   SUBVERSIVE

Jesus Christ, who brought good news,
Talked in the Temple with fellow Jews.

The chief priests' question he struck dumb:
"By what authority art thou come?"

He spoke of the heir of the vineyard known;
The builders rejecting the cornerstone.

The rulers murmured, "He stirs the tribes!"
He was feared by the chief priests and the scribes.

Yet spy how they would, wherever he spoke,
They could not bind his words to the folk.

"For mine is not a God of the dead,
But of the living," Jesus said.

"Beware the long-robed scribes men greet,
Beware the synagogue's highest seat,

"'Ware those who make long prayers for their ease!
The widow's house is devoured by these."

He said, "Great earthquakes yet shall be,
Famine and pestilence fearfully,

Portents from heaven, tyrants risen,
My chosen people cast in prison.

There shall be signs in the sun and moon;
Distress of nations falling soon;

The world in terrible danger taken,
The powers of heaven sorely shaken;

But though earth and heaven shall pass away,"
Simply He said, "my word shall stay."

Yet ever the chief priests and the scribes
Sought to kill him who stirred the tribes.

He said, "I drink no fruit of the vine
Till the kingdom of God be thine and thine."

He taught in the Temple, but took the road,
For the free wide air was his abode.

No edifice could hold in fee
The free man out of Galilee.

Sometimes I wonder, "Where is He?"

Reading his word, the heart doth pine,
For along the page his footprints shine

Who walks in haste with a secret golden,
Speaking to us whose eyes are holden.

But when I hear, as their words defame him,
Furious formalists who claim him,

I think what He said at the dark ebb-tide,
"The Son of Man must be crucified."

Yet also he said, ere he hung on tree,
"I in them, and Thou in me!"

And so he came to Gethsemane.

He prayed in the garden with anguished words.
The priests and captains took him with swords.

Those holding him, mocked with a loud oration,
They said, "This fellow perverteth the nation!"

The soldiers struck him and abused him.
The chief priests vehemently accused him.

He had drained the cup his Father poured.
He had said to Peter, "Put up thy sword."

✠

What have we builded after this?
Edifice on edifice.

They may point upward to the sky,
But they do not always edify.

And now our zealotic chiefs of men
Ruthlessly subdue again

Those who speak a word as free
As the stranger out of Galilee,

On whom they spy with steady hate,
Lest God be greater than the State.

Yet still, throughout the world, there stands
His house, that is not made with hands.

William Rose Benét

81.   EVIL DAYS

When He was entering Jerusalem
During that last week
He was hailed with thunderous hosannas;
The people ran in His wake, waving palm branches.

Yet the days were becoming ever more ominous, more grim.
There was no stirring the hearts of men through love:
Their eyebrows knit in disdain.
And now, the epilogue. Finis.

The heavens lay heavy over the houses,
Crushing with all of their leaden weight.
The Pharisees were seeking evidence against Him,
Yet cringed before Him like foxes.

Then the dark forces of the Temple
Gave Him up to be judged by the offscourings.
And, with the same fervor with which they once sang His praises,
Men now reviled Him.

The rabble from the vicinity
Was peering in at the gateway.
They kept jostling as they bided the outcome,
Surging, receding.

The neighborhood crawled with sly whispers
And rumors crept in from all sides.
He recalled the flight into Egypt and His childhood
But recalled them now as in a dream.

He remembered the majestic cliffside in the wilderness
And that exceeding high mountain
Whereon Satan had tempted Him,
Offering Him all the kingdoms of the world.

And the marriage feast at Cana
And the guests in great admiration over the miracle.
And the sea on which, in a mist,
He had walked to the boat as if over dry land.

And the gathering of the poor in a hovel
And His going down into a cellar by the light of a taper
Which had suddenly gone out in affright
When the man risen from the dead was trying to get to his feet.

Boris Pasternak
tr. *from the Russian by Bernard Guilbert Guerney*

82.   THE LAST SUPPER

I

Apostles of the hidden sun
Are come unto the room of breath

Hung with the banging blinds of death,
The body twelve, the spirit one,
Far as the eye, in earth arrayed,
The night shining, the supper laid.

II

The wine shone on the table that evening of history
Like an enormous ruby in the bauble and mystery.

In the glowing walls of the flickering decanter
There moved His face as at the world's center.

The hands of Judas showed up red and hurried
And the light hit them so, like a cross carried.

The faces of the others were there and moving
In the crystal of the dome, swiftly hovering.

The saints, under a lens, shrunken to pigmies,
Gesticulated in birds or in colored enigmas.

Outside there was a storm, the sound of temblors,
The blood bubbled and sprang into the tumblers.

When the morning came like a white wall of stone,
The day lay in the glass and the blood was gone.

                                        Oscar Williams

83.   THE LAST SUPPER

They are gathered, astounded and disturbed,
round him who, like a sage resolved to his end,
takes himself away from those he belonged to,
and who alien past them flows.
The old loneliness comes over him
that reared him to the doing of his deep acts;

now again will he wander through the olive grove,
and those who love him will take flight before him.

He has summoned them to the last supper
and (as a shot scatters birds out of the sheaves)
he scatters their hands from among the loaves
with his word: they fly across to him;
they flutter anxious through the table's round
and try to find a way out. But he
is everywhere like a twilight-hour.

> Rainer Maria Rilke
> tr. M. D. Herter Norton

84.   GARDEN OF GETHSEMANE

The turn in the road was illumined
By the indifferent glimmer of the remote stars.
The road led around the Mount of Olives;
Below, in its valley, the Brook Kedron ran.

Halfway, the small meadow dipped in a sharp break;
Beyond it began the great Milky Way,
While the silver-gray olives still strained forward
As if to stride onward upon empty air.

Furthest away was someone's garden plot.
He left His disciples outside the stone fence
Saying, "My soul is exceeding sorrowful, even unto death;
Tarry ye here, and watch with me."

He had rejected without resistance
Dominion over all things and the power to work miracles,
As though these had been His only on loan
And now was as all mortals are, even as we.

Night's distance seemed the very brink
Of annihilation, of nonexistence.

The universe's span was void of any life;
The garden only was a coign of being.

And peering into these black abysses—
Void, without end and without beginning—
His brow sweating blood, He pleaded with His Father
That this cup of death might pass from Him.

Having eased His mortal anguish through prayer,
He left the garden. Beyond its wall His disciples,
Overcome with sleep, sprawled on the ground
In the wayside feathergrass.

He awakened them: "God hath granted you to live
During my days on earth, and yet you lie there sprawling.
Behold, the hour is at hand, and the Son of Man
Shall betray Himself into the hands of sinners."

He had scarcely spoken when, coming from none knew where,
A throng of slaves sprang up, a host of vagrant men
With swords and torches, and at their head stood Judas
With the perfidious kiss writhing on his lips.

Peter drew sword and thrust the cutthroats back
And struck a man and smote off his ear.
Whereon he heard, "No metal can resolve dissension.
Put up thy sword again into his place.

Thinkest thou my Father would not send
Sky-darkening hosts of winged legions to my succor?
And without harming even a hair of mine
My enemies would scatter, leaving no trace behind.

But now the book of life has reached a page
Which is more precious than are all the holies.
That which was written now must be fulfilled.
Fulfilled be it, then. Amen.

Seest thou, the passing of the ages is like a parable
And in its passing it may burst to flame.
In the name, then, of its awesome majesty
I shall, in voluntary torments, descend into my grave.

I shall descend into my grave. And on the third day rise again.
And, even as rafts float down a river,
So shall the centuries drift, trailing like a caravan,
Coming for judgment, out of the dark, to me."

Boris Pasternak
tr. from the Russian by Bernard Guilbert Guerney

85.   THE GARDEN OF OLIVES

He went up under the gray foliage
all gray and merging with the olive lands
and laid his forehead that was full of dust
deep in the dustiness of his hot hands.

After everything this. And this was the end.
Now I must go, while I am turning blind,
and why dost Thou so will, that I must say
Thou art, when I myself do no more find Thee.

I find Thee no more. Not within me, no.
Not in the others. Not within this rock.
I find thee no more. I am alone.

I am alone with all mankind's grief,
which I through Thee to lighten undertook,
Thou who art not. O nameless shame. . . .

Later it was said: an angel came—.

Why an angel? Alas it was the night
leafing indifferently among the trees.

The disciples stirred in their dreams.
Why an angel? Alas it was the night.

The night that came was no uncommon night;
hundreds like it go by.
Then dogs sleep, and then stones lie.
Alas a sad night, alas any night
that waits till it be morning again.

For angels come not to such suppliants,
and nights do not round about such grow large.
Who lose themselves by all things are let go,
and they are abandoned of their fathers
and shut out of their mothers' hearts.

Rainer Maria Rilke
tr. from the German by M. D. Herter Norton

86. GOLGOTHA

Take me down from this cross, for now my body is broken,
And the feet pierced and the hands pierced, and in my side
The heart fails me—it breaks, and the words that I have spoken
Are as nothing: you were deceived in me, and I have lied.

Take me down, lower me from the tree—yet slowly,
My spirit is heavy and my heart sick, my flesh is sore
From the bruising and from the bitter scourging, and the holy
Dream that was in me once is in me now no more.

There is no virtue left in me, there is not any
Hope left in me to help you: if it must be done,
As it was written in the old days, that one for many
Should be uplifted—truly, I am not that one.

The nails bite deep into my flesh—shall I endure it
Longer? No longer! Loose me, take me down and lay

My body in the cool tomb—and seal it up, secure it
Against the faces, the proud faces, the blind day.

For I am tired and have need of night to cover me,
And secrecy wherein to hide my shame, and deep
Silence and solitude forevermore, and over me
Darkness—and a lone resting-place and a long sleep.

And yet, nevertheless, perhaps a little longer
I may endure it. Father, if this thing must be,
Give me the strength! Ah yet, perhaps, a little longer—
I will pour out Thy love upon them in my agony.

John Hall Wheelock

87.   THE KILLING

That was the day they killed the Son of God
On a square hill-top by Jerusalem.
Zion was bare, her children from their maze
Sucked by the demon curiosity
Clean through the gates. The very halt and blind
Had somehow got themselves up to the hill.

After the ceremonial preparation,
The scourging, nailing, nailing against the wood,
Erection of the main-trees with their burden,
While from the hill rose an ancestral wailing,
They were there at last, high up in the soft spring day.

We watched the writhings, heard the moanings, saw
The three heads turning on their separate axles
Like broken wheels left spinning. Round *his* head
Was loosely bound a crown of plaited thorn
That hurt at random, stinging temple and brow
As the pain swung into its envious circle.
In front the wreath was gathered in a knot

That as he gazed looked like the last stump left
Of a death-wounded deer's great antlers. Some
Who came to stare grew silent as they looked,
Indignant or sorry. But the hardened old
And the hard-hearted young, although at odds
From the first morning, cursed him with one curse,
Having prayed for a Rabbi or an armed Messiah
And found the Son of God. What use to them
Was a God or a Son of God? Of what avail
For purposes such as theirs? Beside the cross-foot,
Alone, four women stood and did not move
All day. The sun revolved, the shadows wheeled,
The evening fell. His head lay on his breast,
But in his breast they watched his heart move on
By itself alone, accomplishing its journey.
Their taunts grew louder, sharpened by the knowledge
That he was walking in the park of death,
Far from their rage. Yet all grew stale at last,
Spite, curiosity, envy, hate itself.
They waited only for death and death was slow
And came so quietly they scarce could mark it.
They were angry then with death and death's deceit.

I was a stranger, could not read these people
Or this outlandish deity. Did a God
Indeed in dying cross my life that day
By chance, he on his road and I on mine?

                                                    Edwin Muir

88.   IT IS FINISHED

There was a trampling of horses from Calvary,
Where the armed Romans rode from the mountainside;
Yet, riding, they dreamed of the soul that could rise free
Out of the bruised breast and the arms nailed wide.

There was a trampling of horses from Calvary,
And the long spears glittered into the night;
Yet, riding they dreamed of the will that dared to be
When the head bowed and the heavens were rent with light.

The eyelids that closed over sleep like folded wings,
And the proud mouth that kissed death with the cry
"Father, forgive them"—silently these things
They remembered, riding down from Calvary.

And Joseph, when the sick body was lowered slowly,
Folded it in a white cloth without seam—
The indomitable brow, inflexible and holy,
And the sad breast that held the immortal dream,

And the feet that could not walk, and the piercèd hand,
And the arms that held the whole world in their embrace.
But Mary, beside the cross-tree, could not understand,
Looking upon the tired, human face.

John Hall Wheelock

89.   UNKEPT GOOD FRIDAYS

There are many more Good Fridays
Than this, if we but knew
The names, and could relate them,
Of men whom rulers slew
For their goodwill, and date them
As runs the twelvemonth through.

These nameless Christs' Good Fridays,
Whose virtues wrought their end,
Bore days of bonds and burning,
With no man to their friend,
Of mockeries, and spurning;
Yet they are all unpenned.

When they had their Good Fridays
Of bloody sweat and strain
Oblivion hides. We quote not
Their dying words of pain,
Their sepulchres we note not,
Unwitting where they have lain.

No annual Good Fridays
Gained they from cross and cord,
From being sawn asunder,
Disfigured and abhorred,
Smitten and trampled under:
Such dates no hands have scored.

Let be. Let lack Good Fridays
These Christs of unwrit names;
The world was not even worthy
To taunt their hopes and aims,
As little of earth, earthy,
As his mankind proclaims.

Thomas Hardy

90.   CRUCIFIX

Here is this silver crucifix, to recall
Immortal agony: the mortality of the immortal;
Christ crucified again, but painlessly, in effigy;
All wrought to grace; anguish translated to beauty, suffering feigned
in calm silver.
Look at this, then think of the actual scene:
Friday, Friday the thirteenth, as some think,
Hot and bright at first, but gradually darkening and chilling;
The rock and sway of a great packed crowd.
A crowd like any other that comes to witness executions,
With market-baskets and bundles and purses and other tokens of lives
that would be resumed

After this interruption; a crowd with children and dogs
Crawling in and out through the forest of legs.
Think of the straining, the craning to see as hammers and nails
Behaved after the fashion of hammers and nails,
Though the nails went through veins and flesh and wedged bones
apart.
And then the cross raised, the third of that day, displaying to all eyes
(Eyes glittering or sombre, lust-lit or horror-struck, but mostly
curious)
The head, turning slowly from side to side,
As always with the pinned or the impaled,
The eyes already rapt with suffering,
The hands nailed like frogs to the rough cross-timber,
The feet spiked to the foot-block; amid cries and murmurs
The cross raised; and after a little while,
The eyes of the spectators straying, their lips beginning to discuss
other executions, and other things than executions,
The crowd slowly dispersing, the best parts being over,
Leaving only a few whispering at the foot of the cross in the gathering
dark, and the Roman soldiers,
To whom this was another crucifixion,
Glad to relax after the anxieties of maintaining discipline.

Think of the terrible solitude of the Cross:
Of that body shuddering (for it was a body)
And the knees buckling, as they would, till straightened convulsively
In the drag of the body's weight on the hands and the aching arm-pits,
And again and again buckling and straightening, again and again
throughout the long day, as weakness overcomes pain, and pain
weakness.
And the painful thirst of the wounded, worse than the wounds,
And the flies, to whom Christ's blood was as any other,
And worse than all, the fear, the increasing fear
That all had been illusion, save this pain, this death
(For we think that none, not even God, may put on the man-shape
and not feel this fear)
And this in the terrible solitude of the Cross.

Think of this, gaze your fill on it, then remember
It is the Christ that sanctifies the Cross,
Not the Cross, Christ; and remember, it is not
Preëminence in pain that makes the Christ
(For the thieves as well were crucified)
No, but the God head; the untouchable unguessable unsuffering
Immortality beyond mortality,
Which feigns our mortality as this silver feigns it,
And of which we are ignorant as that multitude;
For the pain comes from the humanity; the pain we know;
The agony we comprehend; of the rest, know nothing.

Elder Olson

91.   STILL FALLS THE RAIN

Still falls the Rain—
Dark as the world of man, black as our loss—
Blind as the nineteen hundred and forty nails
Upon the Cross.

Still falls the Rain
With a sound like the pulse of the heart that is changed to the
                                                hammer-beat
In the Potter's Field, and the sound of the impious feet

On the Tomb:
              Still falls the Rain
In the Field of Blood where the small hopes breed and the human
                                                brain
Nurtures its greed, that worm with the brow of Cain.

Still falls the Rain
At the feet of the Starved Man hung upon the Cross.
Christ that each day, each night, nails there, have mercy on us—
On Dives and on Lazarus:
Under the Rain the sore and the gold are as one.

Still falls the Rain—
Still falls the Blood from the Starved Man's wounded Side:
He bears in His Heart all wounds—those of the light that died,
The last faint spark
In the self-murdered heart, the wounds of the uncomprehending
dark,

The wounds of the baited bear—
The blind and weeping bear whom the keepers beat
On his helpless flesh . . . the tears of the hunted hare.

Still falls the Rain—
Then—O Ile leape up to my God: who pulles me doune—
See, see where Christ's blood streames in the firmament:
It flows from the Brow we nailed upon the tree
Deep to the dying, to the thirsting heart
That holds the fires of the world—dark-smirched with pain
As Caesar's laurel crown.

Then sounds the voice of One who like the heart of man
Was once a child who among beasts has lain—
'Still do I love, still shed my innocent light, my Blood, for thee.'

Edith Sitwell

92.   I SEE HIS BLOOD UPON THE ROSE

I see His blood upon the rose
And in the stars the glory of His eyes,
His body gleams amid eternal snows,
His tears fall from the skies.

I see His face in every flower;
The thunder and the singing of the birds
Are but His voice—and carven by His power
Rocks are His written words.

All pathways by His feet are worn,
His strong heart stirs the ever-beating sea,

His crown of thorns is twined with every thorn,
His cross is every tree.

Joseph Plunkett

93.   EASTER HYMN

Out of the cloud my Lord the Sun,
Out of the earth my Lady Spring,
Out of the seed the Princeling green,
Out of the grave my God and King.
Sing, Oh sing.
This is the time of bursting barriers, the ice melting,
Birds singing and winging abroad, the shooting of foliage,
Triumph and joy of earth and heaven both.
Joy, man, with both.
For He our Saviour, God and man,
Is risen from death, Nature's prime law,
Is risen at Nature's festival
Of power; 'twas this He perished for.
Joy therefore man with a double joy; joy in obedience
To the pulse of Earth Mother, leaping and live within us,
But joy in the Christ earth bore but could not fetter,
Whose love home to our Father's house shall win us.

Michael Thwaites

94.   THE THIRD DAY

On what silent feet it comes,
The third day!
No signal or sound,
No stirring above ground.
Evil on its way
Is preceded by crowds
Of menacing purple clouds.
Much pageant for ill,
But why must the herald of good be so still?

No broad avenue, no triumphal gate
Indicate
Imminent joy.
Master, forgive the surprise
Holding our incredulous eyes.
We are so used to pain,
We are so used to grief;
Gain is a hard belief,
Joy is an impossible faith.
But this is no wraith
On the third day!
No sound, no stir—
How could we infer
That it must be so?
Lord, we cannot guess or believe,
We can only know.

Edith Lovejoy Pierce

95.   EASTER SONG

Let the bells of Easter toll,
Christ has risen in my soul!
Hear the choir sing and say,
Christ is in my heart today!
Listen while the word is said,
Christ is risen, I am dead!
Voice and bell and organ roll,
Christ is risen in my soul!

Christ breaks every precious scheme
That I hold against His dream.
Christ gave Paul his badge of 'fool'
For his wisdom and his rule.
Christ paid Pilate's slight esteem
With a strange incessant dream.
Christ gave Judas back his kiss
In the rope's embracing hiss.

Ring it fairly, ring it well,
Christ the clapper, I the bell,
Ring it boldly to the sky,
One must live, 'tis He or I.
As I bury deep my pride,
I set free the Crucified.
Ring me empty, ring me dead,
Make me suffer in His stead!
Beat upon me till I know
Something of His secret woe!
Silence me until I thrill
To the hammer of His will!

Softly ring, He comes to rest
In the quiet of my breast.

Kenneth Leslie

VII   the god of galaxies

"O Light Invisible we praise thee!"

96.   THE GOD OF GALAXIES

The god of galaxies has more to govern
Than the first men imagined, when one mountain
Trumpeted his anger, and one rainbow,
Red in the east, restored them to his love.
One earth it was, with big and lesser torches,
And stars by night for candles. And he spoke
To single persons, sitting in their tents.

Now streams of worlds, now powdery great whirlwinds
Of universes far enough away
To seem but fog-wisps in a bank of night
So measureless the mind can sicken, trying—
Now seas of darkness, shoreless, on and on
Encircled by themselves, yet washing farther
Than the last triple sun, revolving, shows.

The god of galaxies—how shall we praise him?
For so we must, or wither. Yet what word
Of words? And where to send it, on which night
Of winter stars, of summer, or by autumn
In the first evening of the Pleiades?
The god of galaxies, of burning gases,
May have forgotten Leo and the Bull.

But God remembers, and is everywhere.
He even is the void, where nothing shines.
He is the absence of his own reflection
In the deep gulf; he is the dusky cinder
Of pure fire in its prime; he is the place
Prepared for hugest planets: black idea,
Brooding between fierce poles he keeps apart.

Those altitudes and oceans, though, with islands
Drifting, blown immense as by a wind,
And yet no wind; and not one blazing coast
Where thought could live, could listen—oh, what word

Of words? Let us consider it in terror,
And say it without voice. Praise universes
Numberless. Praise all of them. Praise Him.

Mark Van Doren

97. THE PATH OF THE STARS

Down through the spheres that chant the Name of One
   Who is the Law of Beauty and of Light
   He came, and as He came the waiting Night
Shook with the gladness of a Day begun;
And as He came, He said: Thy Will Be Done
   On Earth: and all His vibrant Words were white
   And glistening with silver, and their might
Was of the glory of a rising sun.

Unto the Stars sang out His Living Words
   White and with silver, and their rhythmic sound
     Was as a mighty symphony unfurled;
And back from out the Stars like homing birds
   They fell in love upon the sleeping ground
     And were forever in a wakened world.

Thomas S. Jones, Jr.

98. WITH GOD CONVERSING

Red paths that wander through the gray, and cells
Of strangeness, rutted mouldings in the brain,
Untempered fevers heated by old kills,
By the pampered word, by the pat printed rune,
Unbalanced coil under glaucous blooms of thought,
A turning mind, unmitigated thinking that
Feeds human hunger and eats us alive
While cringing to the death, expecting love,—
Such make the self we are. And do you make it?
And practice on us? For we cannot take it.

Listen. Grow mild before the flicking lash
Seems welded to your hand, self-wounder.
What are we, cry we, while our pain leaps lush,
Too jungle thick: the jungle where we wander,
No seeded faith before, nor after, miracle,
Of bidden faith in things unseen, no particle.
For we think only through our troubled selves,
We note the worm that in the apple delves,
See gibbous moons and spots upon the sun,
Speak gibberish, and keep the poor in sin.

Plus birth and death must war-lash winnow
While every pod-burst leaf of May sucks life?
Because we think shall we be less than minnow,
Cat, carrot, rat and bat and such from sense aloof?
What doorless maze is this we wander through
With fuming souls parched of our morning dew?
Reason confounds as it presents to NAUGHT:
Earth worn, man moving into self-made night.
Reason-begotten science sets war's pace
And, civil-mouthed, makes civilization pass.

Created in your image, made up of words,
Till words reduce you to a zero—O,
We, then, reflecting you, are less than birds,
Bugs, or empty dugs, still less than minus no.
There must be something wrong with being wise—
Talking we go, wondering and wandering with woes,
Big thoughts have got us, hence we organize,
Govern our heroes with unmeant yeas and nays,
And breathe in dungeons of our nervous mesh
An air too blank to snare meandering flesh.

Night melting dawn shall turn the renewed sky,
Aurora Borealis and Australis
Fanfaring leap the poles, the moon fall by;
But if our science does not quickly fail us
How long for us will space blue light the dun

Of populaces, while wonderers eye the sun?
The gloomy silhouettes of wings we forged
With reason reasonless, are now enlarged,
The falsified subconscious, beast-a-woken?
We-you? Post-suicides, shall we awaken?

Gene Derwood

99.   ESSAY ON DEITY

God's body is all space.
He is the shifting land
And the lifting seas.
He is the turning wind.
Like waters, all his strange
Substance suffers change
Forever, yet is known
Forever to be one.
Though water dress as blue
Wave or mist or dew
Or ice at the world's end,
It is one element.
Even as waters he
Takes shape of cloud or tree.
I see his essence plain
In transparent rain
And blowing mist: I know
His presence in the snow.

How then, embittered dust
But hostaged unto death,
Thought you to refuse
Your substance to his use?
To every glint of dust,
To every spark of frost,
To every grain of sand
He set his shining hand,

He breathed his shining breath.
How thought you to withstand,
Narrow heart, this power
That touches dimnest star,
That pierces finest seed?
Narrow brain, how thought
Your thinking to shut out
Undimensional Mind?
And you, most narrow sight,
You glass set in the skull,
Reflecting the least leaf,
The littlest flake to fall,
How thought you to lie blind
To that absolute light?

Yet since he everywhere
In water, land, and air
Move as everything—
The gull on stony wing,
The sliding rock, the fish
In the sea's dim mesh—
Then, minute breast of bone,
Behold how all unknown
You drew him home as breath
In crystal lapse and flood.
Heart that refuses God,
You bear him for your blood;
Obdurate mouth, he is
The food that fed your hunger.
Deny him then no longer,
You took him for your bread.
Behold how unaware
In breathing the wild air,
In seeing, being fed,
In knowing even now
These words, this mist and snow,
These birds at the earth's rim,

Whether you will or no,
You have accepted him.

Elder Olson

100.   THE EXCESSES OF GOD

Is it not by his high superfluousness we know
Our God? For to equal a need
Is natural, animal, mineral: but to fling
Rainbows over the rain
And beauty above the moon, and secret rainbows
On the domes of deep sea-shells,
And make the necessary embrace of breeding
Beautiful also as fire,
Not even the weeds to multiply without blossom
Nor the birds without music:
There is the great humaneness at the heart of things,
The extravagant kindness, the fountain
Humanity can understand, and would flow likewise
If power and desire were perch-mates.

Robinson Jeffers

101.   I HEAR AND BEHOLD GOD
IN EVERY OBJECT

I have said that the soul is not more than the body,
And I have said that the body is not more than the soul;
And nothing, not God, is greater to one than one's self is,
And whoever walks a furlong without sympathy, walks to his own
                                    funeral, drest in his shroud,
And I or you, pocketless of a dime, may purchase the pick of the
                                    earth,
And to glance with an eye, or show a bean in its pod, confounds the
                                    learning of all times,
And there is no trade or employment but the young man following it
                                    may become a hero,

And there is no object so soft but it makes a hub for the wheel'd
universe,
And I say to any man or woman, Let your soul stand cool and
composed before a million universes.

And I say to mankind, Be not curious about God,
For I, who am curious about each, am not curious about God;
(No array of terms can say how much I am at peace about God, and
about death.)

I hear and behold God in every object, yet understand God not in
the least,
Nor do I understand who there can be more wonderful than myself.

Why should I wish to see God better than this day?
I see something of God each hour of the twenty-four, and each
moment then;
In the faces of men and women I see God, and in my own face in
the glass;
I find letters from God dropt in the street—and every one is signed
by God's name,
And I will leave them where they are, for I know that wheresoever I
go,
Others will punctually come forever and ever.

Walt Whitman

102. UNISON

There is a secret that the sober mood
Of science misses, it will not be bought
By the contriving mind however shrewd—

Within the cell, within the atom sought,
Within the inner center's whirling rings,
Sits the demonic joy that laughs at thought

And is the face behind the mask of things,
And is the measure of the choric dance,
The music of the song Creation sings.

Who shall unweave the web of Circumstance,
Or trace the pattern in the fugitive
And shifting tapestry of change and chance?

Or, having learned the pattern, who shall give
The answer then? What answer has been given
Ever, to any man, why man should live!

Not in the flesh, not in the spirit even,
Not in the cunning of the brain that rides
In mastery upon the roads of heaven,

Or charts the rhythm of the starry tides,
The answer and the truth are found, but where,
Deep at the very core, the Stranger bides—

And pours his courage through the heart's despair,
And works his healing in the body's wound,
And sheds his glory through the spirit. There

The answer is, the wisdom shall be found,
Which is the answer of the greening tree,
Which is the wisdom of the fruitful ground—

A wisdom older and more wise than we,
Dumb with a secret difficult to tell,
And inarticulate with mystery,

For, to define it, were a miracle.
Oh, not in the low moments but the great
The exultant rhythm is made audible

That sways the music at the heart of Fate,
To which Time in his passage and return
Moves, and the burdened heavens, with their weight

Of suns and planets, are moving as they burn—
The harmony in which all modes are bent
To the one meaning that they all must learn,

Of many and divergent meanings blent,
Of motions intricate and manifold,
With various voices weaving one consent!

Nor is it easy for the mind to hold
The extreme joy of things, or bear for long
The exalted beauty, hidden from of old,

Whose sure intent, immutable and strong,
Secret and tireless and undeterred,
Moves through the mazes of the winding song—

And whosoever in his heart has heard
That music, all his life shall toil to say
The passion of it. But there is no word—

No words are made for it. There is no way.

                                        John Hall Wheelock

103.   PRESENCE

Between me and the moving world's
Variable play of light and sound
You interpose, not less revealed
Because too instant to be known.

Between me and my clearest thought,
My fiercest love, my closest prayer,

Still you contrive to penetrate:
The crux of now, the core of here.

Though I could cross creation out,
Dissolve all elements in one,
Your presence would unvarying wait
Where, from forever, it has been

The silent mover of the play,
The focus of its myriad parts—
Fashioning, for the world and me,
A wholeness from our opposites.

John Moffit

104.   YOU, NEIGHBOR GOD

You, neighbor God, if sometimes in the night
I rouse you with loud knocking, I do so
only because I seldom hear you breathe;
I know: you are alone.
And should you need a drink, no one is there
to reach it to you, groping in the dark.
Always I hearken. Give but a small sign
I am quite near.

Between us there is but a narrow wall,
and by sheer chance; for it would take
merely a call from your lips or from mine
to break it down,
and that all noiselessly.

The wall is builded of your images.

They stand before you hiding you like names,
And when the light within me blazes high
that in my inmost soul I know you by,
the radiance is squandered on their frames.

And then my senses, which too soon grow lame,
exiled from you, must go their homeless ways.

Rainer Maria Rilke
tr. from the German by Babette Deutsch

105.   LOOK, HOW BEAUTIFUL

There is this infinite energy, the power of God forever working—
                    toward what purpose?—toward none.
This is God's will; he works, he grows and changes, he has no object.
No more than a great sculptor who has found a ledge of fine marble,
                    and lives beside it, and carves great images,
And casts them down. That is God's will: to make great things and
                    destroy them, and make great things
And destroy them again. With war and plague and horror, and the
                    diseases of trees and the corruptions of stone
He destroys all that stands. But look how beautiful—
Look how beautiful are all the things that He does. His signature
Is the beauty of things.

Robinson Jeffers

106.   O LIGHT INVISIBLE,
WE PRAISE THEE

O Light Invisible, we praise Thee!
Too bright for mortal vision.
O Greater Light, we praise Thee for the less;
The eastern light our spires touch at morning,
The light that slants upon our western doors at evening,
The twilight over stagnant pools at batflight,
Moon light and star light, owl and moth light,
Glow-worm glowlight on a grassblade.
O Light Invisible, we worship Thee!

We thank Thee for the lights we have kindled,
The light of altar and of sanctuary;

Small lights of those who meditate at midnight
And lights directed through the coloured panes of windows
And light reflected from the polished stone,
The gilded carven wood, the coloured fresco.
Our gaze is submarine, our eyes look upward
And see the light that fractures through unquiet water.
We see the light but see not whence it comes.
O Light Invisible, we glorify Thee!

In our rhythm of earthly life we tire of light.
    We are glad when the day ends, when the play ends; and ecstasy is
                                                    too much pain.
We are children quickly tired: children who are up in the night and
    fall asleep as the rocket is fired; and the day is long for work or play.
We tire of distraction or concentration, we sleep and are glad to
                                                    sleep,
Controlled by the rhythm of blood and the day and the night and
                                                    the seasons.
And we must extinguish the candle, put out the light and relight it;
Forever must quench, forever relight the flame.
Therefore we thank Thee for our little light, that is dappled with
                                                    shadow.
We thank Thee who hast moved us to building, to finding, to
        forming at the ends of our fingers and the beams of our eyes
And when we have built an altar to the Invisible Light, we may set
        thereon the little lights for which our bodily vision is made.
And we thank Thee that darkness reminds us of light.
O Light Invisible, we give Thee thanks for Thy great glory!
                                                    T. S. Eliot

VIII   BROTHERS

"Stranger, may I button-hole you?"

107.   SOMETHING IN COMMON

Stranger, may I button-hole you,
To say a word about the sun;
A dry word in a tanned ear,
Before each goes his way, the one
Northward, with a furnace at his back,
The other south, his front on fire?
Here where we stop, the cooling stack
Is still not cool enough to keep
The scent of hay from boiling over:
And by the bee that staggers near
I see that honey from the clover
Runs in the heat, and slips the sack.

I'll show you, stranger, how to roll you
A devil's rhubarb to a shape
That fits into your threatened nape
And saves a touch of fever-stroke
(You going north) or any other
Mischief to the skin or blood.
Maybe it's madness to have stood
Even a moment in this flame;
But such universal fire
Is something shared. We've had the same
Blinding experience and desire.
My way lies southward. Good day, brother.

Richard Church

108.   THE DIVINE SHIP SAILS
THE DIVINE SEA FOR YOU

Whoever you are! motion and reflection are especially for you; the
divine ship sails the divine sea for you.

Whoever you are! you are he or she for whom the earth is solid and
liquid,

You are he or she for whom the sun and moon hang in the sky,
For none more than you is immortality.

Each man to himself, and each woman to herself, such is the word of
                        the past and present, and the word of immortality;
No one can acquire for another—not one!
No one can grow for another—not one!

The song is to the singer, and comes back most to him;
The teaching is to the teacher, and comes back most to him;
The murder is to the murderer, and comes back most to him;
The theft is to the thief, and comes back most to him;
The love is to the lover, and comes back most to him;
The gift is to the giver, and comes back most to him—it cannot fail;
And no man understands any greatness or goodness but his own, or
                        the indication of his own.

I swear the earth shall surely be complete to him or her who shall be
                        complete!
I swear the earth remains jagged and broken only to him or her who
                        remains jagged or broken!
I swear I begin to see little or nothing in audible words.
All merges toward the presentation of the unspoken meanings of the
                        earth;
Toward him who sings the songs of the Body, and of the truth of the
                        earth;
Toward him who makes the dictionaries of words that print cannot
                        touch.

I see what is better than to tell the best;
It is always to leave the best untold.
The best of the earth cannot be told anyhow—all or any is best;
It is not what you anticipated—it is much nearer to you.

Health to you! Good will to you all! . . .
Whoever you are, now I place my hand upon you, that you be my
                        poem;
I will leave all, and come and make the hymns of you;

I am he who places over you no master, owner, better, beyond what
                                        waits intrinsically in yourself.

Each of us inevitable;
Each of us limitless—each of us with his or her right upon the earth;
Each of us allowed the eternal purports of the earth;
Each of us here as divinely as any is here.

                                        Walt Whitman

109.   THE LITANY OF THE
DARK PEOPLE

Our flesh that was a battle-ground
Shows now the morning-break;
The ancient deities are drowned
For thy eternal sake.
Now that the past is left behind,
Fling wide thy garment's hem
To keep us one with Thee in mind,
Thou Christ of Bethlehem.

The thorny wreath may ridge our brow,
The spear may mar our side,
And on white wood from a scented bough
We may be crucified;
Yet no assaults the old gods make
Upon our agony
Shall swerve our footsteps from the wake
Of Thine toward Calvary.

And if we hunger now and thirst,
Grant our withholders may,
When heaven's constellations burst
Upon Thy crowning day,
Be fed by us, and given to see
Thy mercy in our eyes,

When Bethlehem and Calvary
Are merged in Paradise.

Countee Cullen

110.   FOR MY PEOPLE

For my people everywhere singing their slave songs repeatedly: their
    dirges and their ditties and their blues and jubilees, praying their
    prayers nightly to an unknown god, bending their knees humbly to
                                                              an unseen power;

For my people lending their strength to the years, to the gone years
    and the now years and the maybe years, washing ironing cooking
    scrubbing sewing mending hoeing plowing digging planting pruning
    patching dragging along never gaining never reaping never knowing
                                                    and never understanding;

For my playmates in the clay and dust and sand of Alabama
    backyards playing baptizing and preaching and doctor and jail and
    soldier and school and mama and cooking and playhouse and
        concert and store and hair and Miss Choomby and company;

For the cramped bewildered years we went to school to learn to know
    the reasons why and the answers to and the people who and the
    places where and the days when, in memory of the bitter hours
    when we discovered we were black and poor and small and different
    and nobody cared and nobody wondered and nobody understood;

For the boys and girls who grew in spite of these things to be man
    and woman, to laugh and dance and sing and play and drink their
    wine and religion and success, to marry their playmates and bear
    children and then die of consumption and anemia and lynching;

For my people thronging 47th Street in Chicago and Lenox Avenue
    in New York and Rampart Street in New Orleans, lost disinherited
    dispossessed and happy people filling the cabarets and taverns and

other people's pockets needing bread and milk and shoes and land
    and money and something—something all their own;

For my people walking blindly spreading joy, losing time being lazy,
    sleeping when hungry, shouting when burdened, drinking when
    hopeless, tied and shackled and tangled among ourselves by the
    unseen creatures who tower over us omnisciently and laugh;

For my people blundering and groping and floundering in the dark
    of churches and schools and clubs and societies, associations and
    councils and committees and conventions, distressed and disturbed
    and deceived and devoured by money-hungry glory-craving leeches,
    preyed on by facile force of state and fad and novelty, by false
                                prophet and holy believer;

For my people standing staring trying to fashion a better way from
    confusion, from hypocrisy and misunderstanding, trying to fashion
    a world that will hold all the people, all the faces, all the adams
                    and eves and their countless generations;

Let a new earth rise. Let another world be born. Let a bloody peace
    be written in the sky. Let a second generation full of courage issue
    forth; let a people loving freedom come to growth. Let a beauty
    full of healing and a strength of final clenching be the pulsing in
    our spirits and our blood. Let the martial songs be written, let the
    dirges disappear. Let a race of men now rise and take control.

                                            Margaret Walker

111.   THE   PEBBLE

        If any have a stone to shy,
        Let him be David and not I;
        The lovely shepherd, brave and vain,
        Who has a maggot in the brain,
        Which, since the brain is bold and pliant,
        Takes the proportions of a giant.
        Alas, my legendary fate!

Who sometimes rage, but never hate.
Long, long before the pebble flieth
I see a virtue in Goliath;
Yea, in the Philistine his face,
A touching majesty and grace;
Then like the lights of evening shine
The features of the Philistine
Until my spirit faints to see
The beauty of my enemy.
If any have a stone to fling
Let him be a shepherd-king,
Who is himself so beautiful
He may detest the gross and dull
With holy rage and heavenly pride
To make a pebble sanctified
And feather its course with wings of scorn;
But, from the day that I was born
Until like corn I bow to the sickle,
I am in hatred false and fickle.

I am most cruel to anyone
Who hates me with devotion;
I will not freeze, I will not burn;
I make his heart a poor return
For all the passion that he spends
In swearing we shall never be friends;
For all the pains his passion spent
In hatred I am impotent;
The sad perversity of my mind
Sees in him my kin and kind.
Alas, my shameful heritage,
False in hate and fickle in rage!
Alas, to lack the power to loathe!
I like them each; I love them both;
Philistine and the shepherd-king
They strike the pebble from my sling;
My heart grows cold, my spirit grows faint;
Behold, a hero and a saint

Where appeared, a moment since,
A giant and a heathen prince;
And I am bound and given over
To be no better than a lover.
Alas, who strove as a holy rebel!
They have broke my sling and stole my pebble:
If any have a stone to throw
It is not I, ever or now.

                                        Elinor Wylie

112.   TOLERANCE

"It is a foolish thing," said I,
"To bear with such, and pass it by;
Yet so I do, I know not why!"

And at each cross I would surmise
That if I had willed not in that wise
I might have spared me many sighs.

But now the only happiness
In looking back that I possess—
Whose lack would leave me comfortless—

Is to remember I refrained
From masteries I might have gained,
And for my tolerance was disdained;

For see, a tomb. And if it were
I had bent and broke, I should not dare
To linger in the shadows there.

                                        Thomas Hardy

113.   UNDER ALL CHANGE

Love is not love which altereth.
I know this now.

I know that under all passion and all change,
Under all peace and all distraction of the days that pass,
There will be this.
I know it with the mind's most cold appraising eye,
Dividing truth from wish; dividing
Lie from love; dividing
Thunder of God from drum of the desire.

It is a fixed star . . . and I know,
Down through the spiral rush of days,
Down through the slow dissolving of all years,
Down to the ultimate darkness and the end,
I shall remember your hands and your face,
And your dear voice saying—
"This is my little friend."

Josephine W. Johnson

114.   THE GOOD MAN IN HELL

If a good man were ever housed in Hell
   By needful error of the qualities,
Perhaps to prove the rule or shame the devil,
   Or speak the truth only a stranger sees,

Would he, surrendering quick to obvious hate,
   Fill half eternity with cries and tears,
Or watch beside Hell's little wicket gate
   In patience for the first ten thousand years,

Feeling the curse climb slowly to his throat
   That, uttered, dooms him to rescindless ill,
Forcing his praying tongue to run by rote,
   Eternity entire before him still?

Would he at last, grown faithful in his station,
   Kindle a little hope in hopeless Hell,

And sow among the damned doubts of damnation,
 Since here someone could live and could live well?

One doubt of evil would bring down such a grace,
 Open such a gate, all Eden could enter in,
Hell be a place like any other place,
 And love and hate and life and death begin.

                                        Edwin Muir

115.   ANY HUMAN TO ANOTHER

The ills I sorrow at
Not me alone
Like an arrow,
Pierce to the marrow,
Through the fat
And past the bone.

Your grief and mine
Must intertwine
Like sea and river,
Be fused and mingle,
Diverse yet single,
Forever and forever.

Let no man be so proud
And confident,
To think he is allowed
A little tent
Pitched in a meadow
Of sun and shadow
All his little own.

Joy may be shy, unique,
Friendly to a few,
Sorrow never scorned to speak

To any who
Were false or true.

Your every grief
Like a blade
Shining and unsheathed
Must strike me down.
Of bitter alocs wreathed,
My sorrow must be laid
On your head like a crown.

Countee Cullen

116.   GLASS HOUSES

Learn if you must, but do not come to me
For truth of what your pleasant neighbor says
Behind you of your looks or of your ways,
Or of your worth and virtue generally;
If he's a pleasure to you, let him be—
Being the same to him; and let your days
Be tranquil, having each the other's praise.

Two others once did love each other well,
Yet not so well but that a pungent word
From each came stinging home to the wrong ears.
The rest would be an overflow to tell,
Surely; and you may slowly have inferred
That you may not be here a thousand years.

Edwin Arlington Robinson

117.   THE SUM OF ALL KNOWN REVERENCE

The sum of all known reverence I add up in you whoever you are.
The men who govern are there for you, it is not you who are here

for them. Laws, courts, the forming of States, the charters of cities,
the going and coming of commerce and mail, are all for you.

If you were not breathing and walking here, where would they all be?
The most renowned poems would be ashes; orations and plays
would be vacuums.
Sculpture and monuments and anything inscribed anywhere are
tallied in you.
All architecture is what you do to it when you look upon it.
All music is what awakes from you when you are reminded by the
instruments.
The sun and stars that float in the open air; the apple-shaped earth
and we upon it; the endless pride and outstretching of man;
unspeakable joys and sorrows; the wonder everyone sees in everyone
else he sees, and the wonders that fill each minute of time forever:
It is for you whoever you are; it is no farther from you than your
hearing and sight are from you; it is hinted by nearest, commonest,
readiest.
Old institutions, these arts, libraries, collections, and the practice
handed along in manufactures, will we rate them so high? Will we
rate our cash and business high?
I have no objections, I rate them as high as the highest—then a child
born of a woman and a man I rate beyond all rate.

You consider bibles and religions divine. I do not say they are not
divine; I say they have all grown out of you, and may grow out of
you still.
It is not they who give the life, it is you who give the life.

Walt Whitman

118.   OUT OF WISDOM HAS COME LOVE
From "The Three Taverns"
(St. Paul speaking)

Many with ears
That hear not yet, shall have ears given them,
And then they shall hear strangely. Many with eyes

That are incredulous of the Mystery
Shall yet be driven to feel, and then to read
Where language has an end, and is a veil,
Not woven of our words. Many that hate
Their kind are soon to know that without love
Their faith is but the perjured name of nothing.
I that have done some hating in my time
See now no time for hate; I that have left,
Fading behind me like familiar lights
That are to shine no more for my returning,
Home, friends, and honors,—I that have lost all else
For wisdom, and the wealth of it, say now
To you that out of wisdom has come love,
That measures and is of itself the measure
Of works and hope and faith.

Edwin Arlington Robinson

IX   the heroic in man

"I think continually of those who were truly great"

119.   I THINK CONTINUALLY OF THOSE WHO WERE TRULY GREAT

I think continually of those who were truly great.
Who, from the womb, remembered the soul's history
Through corridors of light where the hours are suns,
Endless and singing. Whose lovely ambition
Was that their lips, still touched with fire,
Should tell of the Spirit, clothed from head to foot in song.
And who hoarded from the Spring branches
The desires falling across their bodies like blossoms.

What is precious is never to forget
The essential delight of the blood drawn from ageless springs
Breaking through rocks in worlds before our earth.
Never to deny its pleasure in the morning simple light
Nor its grave evening demand for love.
Never to allow gradually the traffic to smother
With noise and fog, the flowering of the spirit.

Near the snow, near the sun, in the highest fields,
See how these names are fêted by the waving grass
And by the streamers of white cloud
And whispers of wind in the listening sky,
The names of those who in their lives fought for life,
Who wore at their hearts the fire's centre.
Born of the sun, they travelled a short while toward the sun,
And left the vivid air signed with their honour.

Stephen Spender

120.   LITANY OF THE HEROES

Would I might wake St. Francis in you all,
Brother of birds and trees, God's Troubadour,
Blinded with weeping for the sad and poor;

Our wealth undone, all strict Franciscan men,
Come, let us chant the canticle again
Of mother earth and the enduring sun.
God make each soul the lonely leper's slave;
God make us saints, and brave.

Would we were lean and grim, and shaken with hate
Like Dante, fugitive, o'er-wrought with cares,
And climbing bitterly the stranger's stairs,
Yet Love, Love, Love, divining: finding still
Beyond dark Hell the penitential hill,
And blessed Beatrice beyond the grave.
Jehovah lead us through the wilderness:
God make our wandering brave.

Would I might wake in you the whirlwind soul
Of Michelangelo, who hewed the stone
And Night and Day revealed, whose arm alone
Could draw the face of God, the titan high
Whose genius smote like lightning from the sky—
And shall he mold like dead leaves in the grave?
Nay, he is in us! Let us dare and dare.
God help us to be brave.

Would that in body and spirit Shakespeare came
Visible emperor of the deeds of Time,
With Justice still the genius of his rhyme,
Giving each man his due, each passion grace,
Impartial as the rain from Heaven's face
Or sunshine from the Heaven-enthroned sun.
Sweet Swan of Avon, come to us again.
Teach us to write, and writing, to be men.

Would we were blind with Milton and we sang
With him of uttermost Heaven in a new song,

That men might see again the angel-throng,
And newborn hopes, true to this age, would rise,
Pictures to make men weep for paradise,
All glorious things beyond the defeated grave.
God smite us blind, and give us bolder wings;
God help us to be brave.

Then let us seek out shining Emerson
Teacher of Whitman, and better priest of man,
The self-reliant granite American.
Give us his Heaven-sent right to strike and spare,
Give us the wools and hair-shirts prophets wear,
Then Adam's freedom in the Eden-sun.
God help us make each state an Eden-flower,
And blaze long trails to power.

Would we might drink, with knowledge high and kind,
The hemlock cup of Socrates the king,
Knowing right well we know not anything,
With full life done, bowing before the law,
Binding young thinkers' hearts with loyal awe,
And fealty fixed as the ever-enduring sun—
God let us live, seeking the highest light,
God help us die aright.

Nay, I would have you grand, and still forgotten,
Hid like the stars at noon, as he who set
The Egyptian magic of man's alphabet;
Or that Egyptian, first to dream in pain
That dauntless souls cannot by death be slain—
Conquering for all men then, the fearful grave.
God keep us hid, yet vaster far than death.
God help us to be brave.

                                        Vachel Lindsay

121.   TESTAMENT

(In memory of my father)

His hands worked ceaselessly at the coverlet
Folding and smoothing it again
In that hushed interval between living and dying.
A craftsman's hands, firm knit and sinewy,
That for a lifetime span
Busied with brush and pigment
Disciplined neutral surfaces
To beauty's clarity and proportion.
Now in this time of unaccustomed quiet
Come upon them so suddenly
They wrestle with the idle moment
Urgent to execute
Some artifact to dictates of the mind
That is now moving into a new pattern,
And the sole industry of contemplation.

Since that first precept given in Paradise,
Yaweh to Adam—keep and dress the land—
Work is a blessed thing.
Even after trespass and the shut gate
Labor is holy—
Not sui generis a slavery,
But sign of the liberty of the sons of God;
A dialogue with Him in His creation
Who, by a unique ordering
So fashioned man an intellectual being
Whose singular delight would be
To conspire with Him to help each creature
Attain its end the more abundantly.
Thus the more praised is God.

In the sublime chironomy of toil,
This collusion between creator and his creature,

Hands execute the ineffable purposes,
Make corporate the existential spark
That glows like a Pleiad in the creative mind:
Adam our father, working the recalcitrant glebe
Into soft furrows, the Etruscan's dream
Caught in the fragile vase, the medieval soul
Leaping in Chartres.
Rodin, Rouault, Auden, Prokofiev—
Like a little white cloud a concerto springs from the ivory;
And a canticle from the rock of Morningside.

Still, in the execution
The ultimate focus is not upon doing but being;
As in God's cry in *Exodus* to build a tabernacle,
And in shaping of the cosmic habitation
Is builded the great temple of the spirit,
Rarer than shittim wood and onyx stone,
Over which the *Shekinah* shall more than brood,
But live as in His own house.

My father's work is done.
His simple testament
I can well ponder all my days:
Witness by these presents
Of hands so bent on the divine routine
In their long dialogue with reality
That they refuse to rest
Even as the last darkness gathers in,
And the spirit entering a new dimension
Has left them orphans.
For man the maker lives in no cactus land;
His hands are not impersonal,
But keep the gladdening rhythms of toil
Even as God's hand closes over them
And the great door of death swings sharply
Into the endless Sabbath.

There is no opposition between work and contemplation,
In the sweat of his brow man lives and loves and sings
His ultimate hymn to God.

Sister M. Therése

122. THE EAGLE THAT IS FORGOTTEN

(John P. Altgeld. Born December 30, 1847; died March 12, 1902)

Sleep softly . . . eagle forgotten . . . under the stone.
Time has its way with you there, and the clay has its own.

"We have buried him now," thought your foes, and in secret rejoiced.
They made a brave show of their mourning, their hatred unvoiced.
They had snarled at you, barked at you, foamed at you day after day.
Now you were ended. They praised you, . . . and laid you away.

The others that mourned you in silence and terror and truth,
The widow bereft of her crust, and the boy without youth,
The mocked and the scorned and the wounded, the lame and the
poor
That should have remembered forever, . . . remember no more.

Where are those lovers of yours, on what name do they call
The lost, that in armies wept over your funeral pall?
They call on the names of a hundred high-valiant ones,
A hundred white eagles have risen the sons of your sons,
The zeal in their wings is a zeal that your dreaming began
The valor that wore out your soul in the service of man.

Sleep softly . . . eagle forgotten, . . . under the stone,
Time has its way with you there and the clay has its own.
Sleep on, O brave-hearted, O wise man, that kindled the flame—
To live in mankind is far more than to live in a name,
To live in mankind, far, far more . . . than to live in a name.

Vachel Lindsay

123.　FOR SIMONE WEIL

As a shy deer that hurtles into sunlight
From some dark covert, unswervingly
Your being leaped to truth.
Mystic, philosopher, who lived on summits
That brush God's sill
Where nests that brilliant bird that sings
In the bone-caged spirit
When every other bird is still.

Upon your spare, translucent page
Your mind lies luminous as God made it;
Even the heart scooped hollow as a gourd
Comes upon opal-fire
Among the branches of your thought,
Lighting it back to wisdom;
And the most laggard comer
May reap of leaf and bud and flower
An intellectual summer.

Clean of all sophistry
You had no fear of the dark wood,
You had no dreams to break
Who coveted but to take
Your place among the poor who wrest their bread
From the gaunt furrow and their cup of water
From the split rock overhead.

Then share one bright immortal moment
With us who grope in this lost Eden
Frightened and alone—
Show us again that when one asks for bread
God will not give him a stone;
We who have seen our fairest justices
Lie as a broken toy in a child's hand,
Seek a word, a face, a season
That will transmute the whole,

When the blessed slavery of affliction
Loses one half his soul.

Then fix our eyes upon that dazzling point
Your philosophers dared not see,
Where creator and creation intersect
At the cross-branched tree;
Quicken our feet upon the stair you took
Past reason's naked rafter
As you stumbled toward the last long certitude—
Neither before nor after
Did your rich heart know loss;
If you stopped short of thresholds, did it matter,
If Love leaned down and lifted you across?

                              Sister M. Therése

124. THE WHITE-HAIRED MAN

For Richard Cabot

This man sowed faith wherever he moved.
It was in his hand when he held yours at meeting.
Never so called out of yourself, never so loved
Were you or anyone as by this man in greeting.

For he kept nothing of the thirsting flood.
It poured through him unstinted like a river.
A quickening essence transfused through the blood,
Afterwards strength was in you, he the giver.

For this man, each was given holiness in trust,
Each with a secret gift and none the same,
The gift of healing healing because you must,
Because healing was in you in God's name.

Never doubt. Never find it out too late,
But now flower and bear fruit in human meeting.

Love not transcending the person but incarnate
As in his own hand given you in greeting.

                                        May Sarton

125.   THE GIFT TO BE SIMPLE

Breathing something German at the end,
Which no one understood, he died, a friend
    Or so he meant to be, to all of us.
    Only the stars defined his radius;
His life, restricted to a wooden house,
Was in his head. He saw a fledgling fall.
    Two times he tried to nest it, but it fell
Once more, and died; he wandered home again—
We save so plain a story for great men.
    An angel in ill-fitting sweaters,
    Writing children naive letters,
    A violin player lacking vanities,
    A giant wit among the homilies—
We have no parallel to that immense
    Intelligence.

But if he were remembered for the Bomb,
As some may well remember him, such a tomb,
    For one who hated violence and ceremony
    Equally, would be a wasted irony.
He flew to formal heavens from his perch,
A scientist become his own research,
    And even if the flames were never gold
    That lapped his body to an ash gone cold,
    Even if his death no trumpets tolled,
    There is enough of myth inside the truth
    To make a monument to fit him with;
    And since the universe is in a jar,
    There is no weeping where his heavens are,

And I would remember, now the world is less,
    His gentleness.

Howard Moss

126.   SONG

Now let us honor with violin and flute
A woman set so deeply in devotion
That three times blasted to the root
Still she grew green and poured strength out.

Still she stood fair, providing the cool shade,
Compassion, the thousand leaves of mercy,
The cherishing green hope. Still like a tree she stood,
Clear comfort in the town and all the neighborhood.

Pure as the tree is pure, young
As the tree forever young, magnanimous
And natural, sweetly serving: for her the song,
    For her all love, all praise,
    All honor, as for trees
    In the hot summer days.

May Sarton

127.   SONG FOR ALL SEAS, ALL SHIPS

1

To-day a rude brief recitative,
Of ships sailing the Seas, each with its special flag or ship-signal;
Of unnamed heroes in the ships—of waves spreading and spreading,
                              far as the eye can reach;
Of dashing spray, and the winds piping and blowing;
And out of these a chant, for the sailors of all nations,
Fitful, like a surge.

Of Sea-Captains, young or old, and the Mates—and of all intrepid
                                                            Sailors;
Of the few, very choice, taciturn, whom fate can never surprise, nor
                                                       death dismay,
Picked sparingly, without noise, by thee, old Ocean—chosen by thee,
Thou Sea, that pickest and cullest the race, in Time, and unitest
                                                          Nations!
Suckled by thee, old husky Nurse—embodying thee!
Indomitable, untamed as thee.

(Ever the heroes, on water or on land, by ones or twos appearing,
Ever the stock preserved, and never lost, though rare—enough for
                                                    seed preserved.)

2

Flaunt out, O Sea, your separate flags of nations!
Flaunt out, visible as ever, the various ship-signals!
But do you reserve especially for yourself, and for the soul of man,
                                        one flag above all the rest,
A spiritual woven Signal, for all nations, emblem of man elate above
                                                            death,
Token of all brave captains, and all intrepid sailors and mates,
And all that went down doing their duty;
Reminiscent of them—twined from all intrepid captains, young or
                                                              old;
A pennant universal, subtly waving, all time, o'er all brave sailors,
All seas, all ships.

                                                     Walt Whitman

128.   UPSTREAM

        The strong men keep coming on.
        They go down shot, hanged, sick,
            broken.
        They live on fighting, singing,
            lucky as plungers.

The strong mothers pulling them
    on . . .
The strong mothers pulling them
    from a dark sea, a great prairie,
    a long mountain.
Call hallelujah, call amen, call
    deep thanks.
The strong men keep coming on.

Carl Sandburg

129. TO HIM THAT WAS CRUCIFIED

My spirit to yours, dear brother;
Do not mind because many, sounding your name, do not understand
                                                            you;
I do not sound your name, but I understand you, (there are others
                                                            also;)
I specify you with joy, O my comrade, to salute you, and to salute
    those who are with you, before and since—and those to come also,
That we all labor together, transmitting the same charge and suc-
                                                            cession;
We few, equals, indifferent of lands, indifferent of times;
We, enclosers of continents, all castes—allowers of all theologies,
Compassionaters, perceivers, rapport of men,
We walk silent among disputes and assertions, but reject not the
                                    disputers, nor any thing that is asserted;
We hear the bawling and din—we are reach'd at by divisions,
                            jealousies, recriminations on every side,
They close peremptorily upon us, to surround us, my comrade,
Yet we walk unheld, free, the whole earth over, journeying up and
    down, till we make our ineffaceable mark upon time and the
                                                    diverse eras,
Till we saturate time and eras, that the men and women of races,
    ages to come, may prove brethren and lovers, as we are.

Walt Whitman

X   the WAR GOD

"Let law be father of our peace"

130. THE WAR GOD

Why cannot the one good
Benevolent feasible
Final dove, descend?

And the wheat be divided?
And the soldiers sent home?
And the barriers torn down?
And the enemies forgiven?
And there be no retribution?

Because the conqueror
Is victim of his own power
That hammers his heart
From fear of former fear—
When those he now vanquishes
Destroyed his hero-father
And surrounded his cradle
With fabled anguishes.

Today his day of victory
Weeps scalding lead anxiety
Lest children of these slain
Prove dragon teeth (sown
Now their sun goes down)
To rise up one morning
Stain the sky with blood
And avenge their fathers again.

The defeated, filled with lead,
On the helpless field,
May dream the pious reasons
Of mercy, but alas
They know what they did
In their own high seasons.

The world is the world
And not the slain

Nor the slayer, forgive.
There's no heaven above
To make passionate histories
End with endless love.
Yet under wild seas
Of chafing despairs
Love's need does not cease.

Stephen Spender

131.   CHIVALRY

I dreamed I saw that ancient Irish queen,
Who from her dun, as dawn had opened wide,
Saw the tall foemen rise on every side,
And gazed with kindling eye upon the scene,
And in delight cried, "Noble is their mien."
"Most kingly are they," her own host replied,
Praising the beauty, bravery, and pride
As if the foe their very kin had been.
And then I heard the unnumberable hiss
Of human adders, nation with poisonous breath
Spitting at nation, as if the dragon rage
Would claw the spirit, and I woke at this,
Knowing the soul of man was sick to death
And I was weeping in the iron age.

AE (George William Russell)

132.   "AND THERE WAS A GREAT CALM"

(On The Signing of the Armistice, November 11, 1918)

I

There had been years of Passion—scorching, cold,
And much Despair, and Anger heaving high,
Care whitely watching, Sorrows manifold,

Among the young, among the weak and old,
And the pensive Spirit of Pity whispered, "Why?"

II

Men had not paused to answer. Foes distraught
Pierced the thinned peoples in a brute-like blindness,
Philosophies that sages long had taught,
And Selflessness, were as an unknown thought,
And "Hell!" and "Shell!" were yapped at Lovingkindness.

III

The feeble folk at home had grown full-used
To "dug-outs," "snipers," "Huns," from the war-adept
In the mornings heard, and at evetides perused;
To day-dreamt men in millions, when they mused—
To nightmare-men in millions when they slept.

IV

Waking to wish existence timeless, null,
Sirius they watched above where armies fell;
He seemed to check his flapping when, in the lull
Of night a boom came thencewise, like the dull
Plunge of a stone dropped into some deep well.

V

So, when old hopes that earth was bettering slowly
Were dead and damned, there sounded "War is done!"
One morrow. Said the bereft, and meek, and lowly,
"Will men some day be given to grace? yea, wholly,
And in good sooth, as our dreams used to run?"

VI

Breathless they paused. Out there men raised their glance
To where had stood those poplars lank and lopped,

As they raised it through the four years' dance
Of Death in the now familiar flats of France;
And murmured, "Strange, this! How? All firing stopped?"

VII

Aye; all was hushed. The about-to-fire fired not,
The aimed-at moved away in trance-lipped song.
One checkless regiment slung a clinching shot
And turned. The Spirit of Irony smirked out, "What?"
Spoil peradventures woven of Rage and Wrong?"

VIII

Thenceforth no flying fires inflamed the gray,
No hurtlings shook the dewdrop from the thorn,
No moan perplexed the mute bird on the spray;
Worn horses mused: "We are not whipped to-day;"
No weft-winged engines blurred the moon's thin horn.

IX

Calm fell. From Heaven distilled a clemency;
There was peace on earth, and silence in the sky;
Some could, some could not, shake off misery:
The Sinister Spirit sneered: "It had to be!"
And again the Spirit of Pity whispered, "Why?"

Thomas Hardy

133.   ABRAHAM LINCOLN WALKS AT MIDNIGHT

(In Springfield, Illinois)

It is portentous, and a thing of state
That here at midnight, in our little town

A mourning figure walks, and will not rest,
Near the old court-house pacing up and down,

Or by his homestead, or in shadowed yards
He lingers where his children used to play,
Or through the market, on the well-worn stones
He stalks until the dawn-stars burn away.

A bronzed, lank man! His suit of ancient black,
A famous high top-hat and plain worn shawl
Make him the quaint great figure that men love,
The prairie-lawyer, master of us all.

He cannot sleep upon his hillside now.
He is among us:—as in times before!
And we who toss and lie awake for long
Breathe deep, and start, to see him pass the door.

His head is bowed. He thinks on men and kings.
Yea, when the sick world cries, how can he sleep?
Too many peasants fight, they know not why,
Too many homesteads in black terror weep.

The sins of all the war-lords burn his heart.
He sees the dreadnaughts scouring every main,
He carries on his shawl-wrapped shoulders now
The bitterness, the folly and the pain.

He cannot rest until a spirit-dawn
Shall come; —the shining hope of Europe free:
The league of sober folk, the Workers' Earth,
Bringing long peace to Cornland, Alp and Sea.

It breaks his heart that kings must murder still,
That all his hours of travail here for men
Seem yet in vain. And who will bring white peace
That he may sleep upon his hill again?

                                    Vachel Lindsay

134.   A MAN-MADE WORLD

What a wild room
We enter, when the gloom
Of windowless night
Shuts us from the light

In man's black malicious box.
Then a key locks
Us into the utter dark
Where the nerves hark

For the man-made toys
To whirr with wound-up noise.
The siren wails. After
Broomsticks climb air,

Clocks break through springs,
Then the fire bell rings.
From high and low comes,
Rage of the drums.

Ah, what white rays gleaming
Up to the sky's low ceiling!
Ah, what flashes show
A woman who cries: "Oh!"

Thus the world we made
Pays back what we paid;
Thus the dark descends
On our means become our ends.

Stephen Spender

135.   ASKING FOR IT

Lord God whose mercy guards the virgin jungle;
Lord God whose fields with dragon's teeth are farmed;

Lord God of blockheads, bombing-planes, and bungle,
Assist us to be adequately armed.

Lord God of cruelties incomprehensible
And randomized damnations indefensible,
Perfect us in thy tyrannous technique
For torturing the innocent and weak.

God of the dear old Mastodon's morasses
Whose love pervaded pre-diluvial mud,
Grant us the power to prove, by poison gases,
The needlessness of shedding human blood.

Siegfried Sassoon

136.   MUSIC AND DRUM

When men turn mob
Drums throb:
When mob turns men
Music again.

When souls become Church
Drums beat the search:
When Church becomes souls
Sweet music tolls.

When State is the master
Drums beat disaster:
When master is man
Music can.

Each to be one,
Each to be whole,
Body and soul,
Music's begun.

Archibald MacLeish

137. AT A CALVARY NEAR THE ANCRE

One ever hangs where shelled roads part.
    In this war He too lost a limb,
But His disciples hide apart;
    And now the Soldiers bear with Him.

Near Golgotha strolls many a priest,
    And in their faces there is pride
That they were flesh-marked by the Beast
    By whom the gentle Christ's denied.

The scribes on all the people shove
    And bawl allegiance to the state,
But they who love the greater love
    Lay down their life; they do not hate.

                   Wilfred Owen

138. LITANY OF THE LOST

In breaking of belief in human good;
In slavedom of mankind to the machine;
In havoc of hideous tyranny withstood,
And terror of atomic doom foreseen;
Deliver us from ourselves.

Chained to the wheel of progress uncontrolled;
World masterers with a foolish frightened face;
Loud speakers, leaderless and sceptic-souled;
Aeroplane angels, crashed from glory and grace;
Deliver us from ourselves.

In blood and bone contentiousness of nations,
And commerce's competitive re-start,
Armed with our marvellous monkey innovations,

And unregenerate still in head and heart;
Deliver us from ourselves.

Siegfried Sassoon

139. IN TIME OF
"THE BREAKING OF NATIONS"

I

Only a man harrowing clods
In a slow silent walk
With an old horse that stumbles and nods
Half asleep as they stalk.

II

Only thin smoke without flame
From the heaps of couch-grass;
Yet this will go onward the same
Though Dynasties pass.

III

Yonder a maid and her wight
Come whispering by:
War's annals will fade into night
Ere their story die.

Thomas Hardy

140.   PAX NOBISCUM

No longer, Lord, thy sons shall sow
Hatred and death where poppies blow;

Peace out of harrowed lives shall grow—
          Alleluia!

No more shall flares and rockets rain
Pallor on sons and fathers slain;
Justice shall vanquish grief and pain—
          Alleluia!

Peace-Maker, Christ, whose living word
Quieted waves and sheathed the sword,
Show us thy risen spirit, Lord—
          Alleluia!

Till souls of all the crucified
Waken from sea and mountain-side,
Hailing the dream for which they died—
          Alleluia!
                    Earl Marlatt

141. DIRGE FOR THE NEW SUNRISE

(*Fifteen minutes past eight o'clock, on the morning
of Monday the 6th of August, 1945*)

Bound to my heart as Ixion to the wheel,
Nailed to my heart as the Thief upon the Cross,
I hang between our Christ and the gap where the world was lost

And watch the phantom Sun in Famine Street—
The ghost of the heart of man . . . red Cain
And the more murderous brain
Of Man, still redder Nero that conceived the death
Of his mother Earth, and tore
Her womb, to know the place where he was conceived.

But no eyes grieved—
For none were left for tears:

They were blinded as the years
Since Christ was born. Mother or Murderer, you have given or taken
life—
Now all is one!

There was a morning when the holy Light
Was young . . . The beautiful First Creature came
To our water-springs, and thought us without blame.

Our hearts seemed safe in our breasts and sang to the Light—
The marrow in the bone
We dreamed was safe . . . the blood in the veins, the sap in the tree
Were springs of Deity.

But I saw the little Ant-men as they ran
Carrying the world's weight of the world's filth
And the filth in the heart of Man—
Compressed till those lusts and greeds had a greater heat than that
of the Sun.
And the ray from that heat came soundless, shook the sky
As if in search for food, and squeezed the stems
Of all that grows on the earth till they were dry—
And drank the marrow of the bone:
The eyes that saw, the lips that kissed, are gone—
Or black as thunder lie and grin at the murdered Sun.

The living blind and seeing Dead together lie
As if in love . . . There was no more hating then,
And no more love: Gone is the heart of Man.

Edith Sitwell

142.   THE HAND THAT SIGNED
THE PAPER

The hand that signed the paper felled a city;
Five sovereign fingers taxed the breath,

Doubled the globe of dead and halved a country;
These five kings did a king to death.

The mighty hand leads to a sloping shoulder,
The finger joints are cramped with chalk;
A goose's quill has put an end to murder
That put an end to talk.

The hand that signed the treaty bred a fever,
And famine grew, and locusts came;
Great is the hand that holds dominion over
Man by a scribbled name.

The five kings count the dead but do not soften
The crusted wound nor stroke the brow;
A hand rules pity as a hand rules heaven;
Hands have no tears to flow.

Dylan Thomas

143.   THE PEACEFUL SHEPHERD

If heaven were to do again,
And on the pasture bars,
I leaned to line the figures in
Between the dotted stars,

I should be tempted to forget,
I fear, the Crown of Rule,
The Scales of Trade, the Cross of Faith,
As hardly worth renewal.

For these have governed in our lives,
And see how men have warred.
The Cross, the Crown, the Scales may all
As well have been the Sword.

Robert Frost

144.   HOUSEMATES

This little flickering planet
   Is such a lonely spark
Among the million mighty fires
   That blaze in the outer dark,

The homeless waste about us
   Leaves such a narrow span
To this dim lodging for a night,
   This bivouac of man,

That all the heavens wonder
   In all their alien stars
To see us wreck our fellowship
   In mad fraternal wars.

                   Odell Shepard

145.   REMEMBER THY COVENANT

While nations, howling like Lucifer, fall from the hallowed height,
In this hour of curse, in this hour of schism,
Assure us that blood cannot blot out the primal prism,
That decay has not eaten into the norm of light.

Give us to understand that hope is yet allowed,
That smoke will not scorch the heavenly color and form;
Lord, let thy rainbow appear, not after, but during, the storm.
O God, set thy kiss on the cloud!

                   Edith Lovejoy Pierce

146.   LET THERE BE LAW

Wherever earth is home for men,
Beyond what mountains, by what seas,

Let honor and pride live; but now
Let there be law, transcending these.

Let there be law through all the world,
Whose children love their ancient lands.
May that love grow, but in the shade
Of justice's most mighty hands.

Let those be guardians of our strength,
Lest in long anarchy it cease.
May something deathless now be born.
Let law be father of our peace.

                              Mark Van Doren

XI   the church

**"around me surges a miracle of unceasing
birth and glory and death and resurrection"**

147. INCENSE

Think not that incense-smoke has had its day.
My friends, the incense-time has but begun.
Creed upon creed, cult upon cult shall bloom,
Shrine after shrine grow gray beneath the sun.

And mountain-boulders in our ancient West
Shall guard the graves of hermits truth-endowed:
And there the scholar from the Chinese hills
Shall do deep honor, with his wise head bowed.

And on our old, old plains some muddy stream,
Dark as the Ganges, shall, like that strange tide—
(Whispering mystery to half the earth)—
Gather the praying millions to its side,

And flow past halls with statues in white stone
To saints unborn today, whose lives of grace
Shall make one shining, universal church
Where all Faiths kneel, as brothers, in one place.

                                        Vachel Lindsay

148.   TO J. S. BACH

Now, when the smoking ruins smoulder low
Of what was Europe once, and Christendom,
When all Creation groans, and men despair,
While they who speak your language, breathe your air,
Lead on the dreadful night of Antichrist
Victorious through the world, now more than all,
Gentle and mighty heart, to you I turn
To heal my mortal soul with heavenly voice.

For you had breathed your Lord's own pain and joy
—Heart-piercing sorrow, speechless joy serene.
You lived the first bewildering breathless awe

That God should grow in Mary's womb, that night
The angels sang so clear. You felt the nails,
Partook the unutterable "It is fulfilled,"
And laid your Lord to rest, deep tender grief
Big with the Resurrection. You had looked
Into the world's despair and mortal sin
And not despaired, for God so loved the world.

So, in your music's flying counterpoint,
The threads that boldly follow and cross and mingle
And knot themselves, and all at once resolve
Into the absolute close; and so those airs
That comprehend all sorrow, yet are drawn
Out of eternal truth, and good and glad.
O grace of God, that you, who so had seen
Could tell it so to men! Most holy art
Expressing heavenly love to human heart—
The agony and sweat, the cry, the peace
That passed all understanding, Bach, but yours.

Your joy was new forever. When you speak
I feel my soul on wings, sublime, that first
Great Christian morning breaking on the world,
The Daystar that was risen in your heart.

                                        Michael Thwaites

149.   ALL THOSE HYMNINGS UP TO GOD

All those hymnings up to God of Bach and César Franck
Cannot have been lost utterly, been arrows that went wide.
Like homing birds loosed from the hand, beating up through land
                                                            fog,
Have they not circled up above, poised, and found out direction
(The old God gone, the new not yet, but back of all I AM)?

Such cryings-up confound us; I think they are not tangential,
But aimed at a center; I think that the through-road will follow their
                                                            blaze.

No man has handled God, but these men have come nearest.
I trust them more than the foot rule. Bach may yet have been right.

Abbie Huston Evans

150.   SONG UNDER SHADOW

Fear not the despots raging,
The loud and brazen lie,
The blood that unassuaging
Pours down the noonday sky,
What man thou wert that man thou art
For all that they can do.
A door stands open in the heart
And all good things are true.

Then rise with every morning
Thy risen Lord to find.
With fear and hate and scorning
The blind lead on the blind,
But love who has a world apart
Knows all they never knew.
A door stands open in the heart
And all good things are true.

The awful shadow eyeless
May reap the furrow red,
But clear and kind and guileless
The word of love be said.
Crazed captains without course or chart
May curse a frenzied crew—
A door stands open in the heart
And all good things are true.

From roots of darkness springing
The tree of time doth rear,
But I have heard her singing,

My darling and my dear,
O wayward as all song and art
But pristine as the dew,
A door stands open in the heart
And all good things are true.

William Rose Benét

151. WHY SHOULD MEN LOVE THE CHURCH?

It is hard for those who have never known persecution,
And who have never known a Christian,
To believe these tales of Christian persecution.
It is hard for those who live near a Bank
To doubt the security of their money.
It is hard for those who live near a Police Station
To believe in the triumph of violence.
Do you think that the Faith has conquered the World
And that lions no longer need keepers?
Do you need to be told that whatever has been, can still be?
Do you need to be told that even such modest attainments
As you boast of in the way of polite society
Will hardly survive the Faith to which they owe their significance?
Men! polish your teeth on rising and retiring;
Women! polish your fingernails:
You polish the tooth of the dog and the talon of the cat.
Why should men love the Church? Why should they love her laws?
She tells them of Life and Death, and of all that they would forget.
She is tender where they would be hard, and hard where they would
like to be soft.
She tells them of Evil and Sin, and other unpleasant facts.
They constantly try to escape
From the darkness outside and within
By dreaming of systems so perfect that no one will need to be good.
But the man that is will shadow
The man that pretends to be.

And the Son of Man is crucified always
And there shall be Martyrs and Saints.
And if blood of Martyrs is to flow on the steps
We must first build the steps;
And if the Temple is to be cast down
We must first build the Temple.

T. S. Eliot

152. THE SPRINGFIELD OF THE FAR FUTURE

Some day our town will grow old.
"She is wicked and raw," men say,
"Awkward and brash and profane."
But the years have a healing way.
The years of God are like bread,
Balm of Gilead and sweet.
And the soul of this little town
Our Father will make complete.

Some day our town will grow old,
Filled with the fullness of time,
Treasure on treasure heaped
Of beauty's tradition sublime.
Proud and gay and gray
Like Hannah with Samuel blest.
Humble and girlish and white
Like Mary, the manger guest.

Like Mary the manger queen
Bringing the God of Light
Till Christmas is here indeed
And earth has no more of night,
And hosts of Magi come,
The wisest under the sun

Bringing frankincense and praise
For her gift of the Infinite One.

Vachel Lindsay

153. THROUGH THE STRAIGHT PASS OF SUFFERING

Through the straight pass of suffering
The martyrs even trod,
Their feet upon temptation,
Their faces upon God.

A stately, shriven company;
Convulsion playing round,
Harmless as streaks of meteor
Upon a planet's bound.

Their faith the everlasting troth;
Their expectation fair;
The needle to the north degree
Wades so, through polar air.

Emily Dickinson

154.   i am a little church (no great cathedral)

i am a little church (no great cathedral)
far from the splendor and squalor of hurrying cities
—i do not worry if briefer days grow briefest,
i am not sorry when sun and rain make april

my life is the life of the reaper and the sower;
my prayers are prayers of earth's own clumsily striving
(finding and losing and laughing and crying) children
whose any sadness or joy is my grief or my gladness

around me surges a miracle of unceasing
birth and glory and death and resurrection:
over my sleeping self float flaming symbols
of hope, and i wake to a perfect patience of mountains

i am a little church (far from the frantic
world with its rapture and anguish) at peace with nature
—i do not worry if longer nights grow longest;
i am not sorry when silence becomes singing

winter by spring, i lift my diminutive spire to
merciful Him Whose only now is forever:
standing erect in the deathless truth of His presence
(welcoming humbly His light and proudly His darkness)

                                                   e e cummings

155.   THE MOST-SACRED MOUNTAIN

Space, and the twelve clean winds of heaven,
And this sharp exultation, like a cry, after the slow six thousand
                                         steps of climbing!
This is Tai Shan, the beautiful, the most holy.

Below my feet the foot-hills nestle, brown with flecks of green; and
lower down the flat brown plain, the floor of earth, stretches away
                                         to blue infinity.
Beside me in this airy space the temple roofs cut their slow curves
                                         against the sky,
And one black bird circles above the void.

Space, and the twelve clean winds are here;
And with them broods eternity—a swift, white peace, a presence
                                         manifest.
The rhythm ceases here. Time has no place. This is the end that has
                                         no end.

Here when Confucius came, a half a thousand years before the
            Nazarene, he stepped, with me, thus into timelessness.
The stone beside us waxes old, the carven stone that says: *On this*
spot once Confucius stood and felt the smallness of the world below.

The stone grows old.
Eternity
Is not for stones.
But I shall go down from this airy space, this swift white peace, this
            stinging exultation;
And time will close about me, and my soul stir to the rhythm of
            the daily round.
Yet, having known, life will not press so close, and always I shall feel
            time ravel thin about me;
For once I stood
In the white windy presence of eternity.

Eunice Tietjens

156. THE TEMPLE

Your clear and living voice among the ruins,
Your stern voice commanding the stones to stand upright,
I heard it in the hollow where I was hidden,
In the broken shaft of marble that was once a pillar for the temple,
And now a cave for the swallows.

I had come there because of a certain beauty,
—The carving of an acanthus leaf,
The stone face of a child, and the smell of incense from the stones,
And when I heard your voice I was afraid.

I came into the hot gold light,
The sun on the white marble against a blue sky,
A white and glaring light on all the hills:
And you were there, walking among the ruins,
Tracing the ancient pattern of the stones,

And when I saw your eyes I was afraid.
  We are afraid of the living,
  We are afraid of the restorers,
  We are afraid of those who come with the hammer and nails in
                                                   His name.
O harsh and beautiful voice among the ruins,
Strong and uncompromising and stern,
Saying,
            "My house shall be called a house of prayer,
            But ye have made it a den of thieves . . .
            The stones are broken, and the worshipers are dead,
            —But the marble is not lost!"

                                          Josephine W. Johnson

157.   THE CHURCH

    This autumn day the new cross is set up
    On the unfinished church, above the trees,
    Bright as a new penny, tipping the tip
    Of the elongated spire in the sunny breeze,
    And is at ease;
    Newcomer suddenly, calmly looking down
    On this American university town.

    Someone inside me sketches a cross—askew,
    A child's—on seeing that stick crossed with a stick,
    Some simple ancestor, perhaps, that knew,
    Centuries ago when all were Catholic,
    That this archaic trick
    Brings to the heart and the fingers what was done
    One spring day in Judea to Three in One;

    When God and Man in more than love's embrace,
    Far from their heaven and tumult died,
    And the holy Dove fluttered above the place
    Seeking its desolate nest in the broken side,

And Nature cried
To see Heaven doff its glory to atone
For man, lest he should die in time, alone.

I think of the Church, that stretched magnificence
Housing the crib, the desert, and the tree,
And the good Lord who lived on poverty's pence
Among the fishermen of Galilee,
Courting mortality,
And schooled himself to learn his human part:
A poor man skilled in dialectic art.

What reason for that splendour of blue and gold
For One so great and poor He was past all need?
What but impetuous love that could not hold
Its storm of spending and must scatter its seed
In blue and gold and deed,
And write its busy Books on Books of Days
To attempt and never touch the sum of praise.

I look at the church again, and yet again,
And think of those who house together in Hell,
Cooped by ingenious theological men
Expert to track the sour and musty smell
Of sins they know too well;
Until grown proud, they crib in rusty bars
The Love that moves the sun and the other stars.

Yet fortune to the new church, and may its door
Never be shut, or yawn in empty state
To daunt the poor in spirit, the always poor.
Catholic, Orthodox, Protestant, may it wait
Here for its true estate.
All's still to do; roof, window and wall are bare.
I look, and do not doubt that He is there.

                                        Edwin Muir

158.   CEREMONY FOR BIRTH
AND NAMING

The parents or sponsors shall present themselves
with the child before the Speaker, who shall say:

In all this world of visible images
There is no music, neither shadow of sound
Nor gladness nor a glory to be found
Able to yield us, out of loveliness,
The life we dream, the breath that we pursue.
But still returns the dreamer to the day;
The child again, the morning strength to woo
Out of the over and the under heaven
The song that from our wearier reach withdrew;
The dawn returns, the ancient dark is driven
Forward and from the silence rolls the stone away.

Consider well your ways and lives,
You gardeners of the precious seed.
As brief attenders of the need,
Draw honey from the upper hives,
Make sweet the weather for the flower;
Withdraw the bonds and set it free.
You shall be watchers for an hour,
But it shall never cease to be.

  I ask therefore:
Will you be mindful of your care,
Knowing you are, through him, of those
Who leave their colors in the air
When you are dust and he a rose?

(The parent answers)

Speaker:

Will you take thought before you find
The words to curb his longing will,

And from commands awhile be still,
Considering which of you is blind?

(*The parent answers*)

Speaker:

And who shall say what he must be
Who by your folly may not fly
Or, long be hindered from the sky
Or, shore-bound, never know the sea?

Make him the keeper of the key
To lock or hold in stern array
The urgent fiber of his clay
And send his ranging spirit free.

In the three names of Love, Light, and your
Divine Humanity I name you—

Ridgely Torrence

159. PSALM

I proclaim Thee great and wonderful,
Not because Thou hast made the sun to avail by day
And the stars to avail by night;
Not because Thou hast made the earth and all that is therein,
The fruits of the field, the flowers, the cinemas, the locomotives;
Not because Thou hast made the sea and all that is therein,
The animals and plants, submarines and sirens;
I proclaim Thee great and eternally wonderful
Because Thou makest Thyself tiny in the Eucharist,
So tiny that I, weak and wretched, am able to contain Thee! . . .

Murilo Mendes
tr. from the Spanish by Dudley Poore

160.   FOR A CHRISTENING

The Word shines still
Locked in dumb stone. We approach
The cloistral, chill
Shell that no touch
May take from its own source, its secret rill.

Cupped in this crust
Of crumbling age, light lingers
Liquid in stone. Ah, trust
Your christener's fingers,
Child, and receive our homage, as is just.

Here let him place,
Held in the slanting light,
Your head, touch water, trace
Your name, and write
The effective seal by which men come to grace.

By this one way
They who are dead live more.
This day is still their day
Who went before,
And you their hope, in the sun's moving ray.

Worshippers here,
We are come to see that prism
Take fire, where Christ's own tear
In your baptism
Consecrates, first each drop, then all the sphere.

No future fate
Dismays us where we stand.
The centre is our state
Who hold time's sand
In scales of worship, though it falls by weight.

Of radiant love,
Given starlike without stint
By Father, Son, and Dove,
Take now the print
Which death shall not obliterate, nor time move.

Seeing lives go by
Unlit, the Father chose
That His own Son should die
And His eyes close
On truth, to make a new theology.

Even as He fell
With sabachthani cries
To those three days in hell,
So must your eyes
Close, for three seconds now, to be made well.

Dive, then: receive
This water with our prayer,
That, when the stunned drops leave
Love's image there,
A cloth by pressure may your life reprieve.

For time's old beat
Must change to music when
Fly to His steadfast feet
The souls of men,
And lightning play on every winding-sheet.

So raised, learn this:
To admire a paradox
Is not enough. It is
Lightning that rocks
The shroud itself, if our own loss we kiss.

Then, then alone
We live, when our lives take

That brightness for their own.
So sink; then wake,
Shining, being raised, where holy water shone.

Vernon Watkins

161.   THE CONTEMPLATIVE

He walks where clean lakes lie
At the mind's center; fleeing the laughter
Of gaudy Arab counters
He trades in marts of silence purchasing
With the sole coin of love,
Pity in baskets, peace in wineskins
For the starved prisoners at the broken gate.

His life is a paradox.
Drained empty as the crumpled jugs that wait
At the forsaken cisterns,
He brims with the strange sweetness
Of dripping honeycomb that damps and cools
The spirit's caustic crust.

Distance is ridiculous; he takes the Atlantic
In prayer's bright syllable,
And owns the islands of the tropic seas;
Blinded to multitudes he sees each man
A Christ-face pleading toward him;
And he folds his brothers pitiful to his side
In one white pleat of his robe.

His prayer is inarticulate.
Words lost all pertinence and definition
As a secret, brilliant worm
That tunnels tracks of fire through all his being
Shatters the bright phrase like an ancient wall
Struck by a hurricane, and he is dumb
As one that stood on Pilate's polished stair.

Thus from the simple letter in my hand
I enter worlds of knowledge,
And learn of an industry that fills
Moment to moment endlessly,
For which one formula suffices:
A Word on the lips that never passes them,
And in the heart the total acquiescence
That softly, effortlessly
Slips the catch that opens the soul to love.

Sister M. Therése

XII ꝺoubt, satan, anꝺ sin

"Sir, I commend to you the spirit of Lucifer"

162.   PRAISE DOUBT

Praise the good angel doubt,
Guardian of us that walk
On the deep waters of this world.

Praise him. He never rests,
However weary the way
Over these dark, salt, dangerous meadows.

Do not look down, he says;
Beware with me and the sun
Of faith's innumerable caverns.

Monsters can be there.
You will have plenty of time.
Too soon descending, you are devoured.

Praise him. He believes
In the long day we are given.
Praise him. He dances upon the whitecaps.

                                        Mark Van Doren

163.   DIVINE POEMS: 45

Sir, I commend to you the spirit
Of Lucifer, who was most beautiful
And wore in that proud skull
Rebellion like a jewel exquisite;
I adjure you to meekly admit
That seething genius pre-punctual
Foreword to all the historical:
I beg you to give him his meet.

Brightest of archangels and brightest
Of demons—proud, incomparable Lucifer!
I alone of all men remember

And praise that magnificent zest
That sent God frantic to abuse
And doom this First, pioneering Genius.

                             José Garcia Villa

164.   WHEN SATAN FELL

When Satan fell, he only fell
because the Lord Almighty rose a bit too high,
a bit beyond himself.

So Satan only fell to keep a balance.
"Are you so lofty, O my God?
Are you so pure and lofty, up aloft?
Then I will fall, and plant the paths to hell
with vines and poppies and fig-trees
so that lost sons may eat grapes
and the moist fig
and put scarlet buds in their hair on the way to hell,
on the way to dark perdition."
And hell and heaven are the scales of the balance of life
which swing against each other.

                             D. H. Lawrence

165.   LUCIFER

The king of hell came singing
    Down through the wolds of world;
I heard his harness ringing
    And his volted lightning hurled;
He moved like storm on the midnight
    And struck like a lash uncurled.

My names, he sang, are Lucifer,
    And youth and the devil in man;

They have called me rebel, fire-bringer,
   I am read out of heart and clan—
But the mornings of all the years are mine
   To take them when I can.

The greybeard gods whisper and darken,
   Binding with oath and spell;
I have not heard them, I will not hearken;
   They have no power over hell.
They are but Lucifers grown older,
   Holding what is, is well.

Yet though I trample them down in thunder
   And my treason is law, and my fame
Be as the gods', still from under
   Beats white hell in flame;
And my son Prometheus shall rise against me
   Armored, bearing my name.

Maxwell Anderson

166. OUR FATHER

It is so many ages now since He
Would let the righteous and unrighteous see
That He is God, and anxious about men:
He was a different sort of parent then.

Himself He made His grim chastisement sure;
Himself put up rewards that would endure—
Who set keen eyes on Adam; branded Cain,
Told Noah how to save the world from rain.

Where is He, who with judgment so direct
Gave plans of temples like an architect?
And He, who slowly speaking through the hush

Let flame His bright assurance from a bush?
He that with manna sweet His children fed?
For now they wonder if He's interested.
He summons them no more by name, at night—
He may not even know their names aright!

If any hear His words, they say that He
Speaks lately with a touch of irony—
They say they feel unfathered, left alone,
Hurt by the indifference of His tone.

Roberta Teale Swartz

167.   INVOCATION

O world watched over by the cold moon and the mindless stars,
Earth whereon we accumulate, wherein we culminate,
Out of whose blind and bitter womb with its ancient scars
We emerged, and at the touch of time disintegrate:

Our cycle is not the same as that of grasses sown
In their season under ground. We are never the same
Selves after sowing. Though the cast seeds be our own,
Each harvest is another number, another name.

For though we give ourselves to earth again and again,
What springs from it? Nothing of all that we have lost.
We sow ourselves in sorrow forever, yet we remain:
The lowliest weed could tell at what terrible cost.

Carleton Drewry

168.   CANT

What cant, oh, what hypocrisy
Is centred in this life of man!

Self-preservation is his God,
　And has been, since his life began.
He sits to breakfast with no care
　Of others that have none;
He keeps more idle rooms than two,
　While families live in one;
He saves his gold, and yet he sees
　Others without a penny;
He hoards his clothes, and knows full well
　Of children without any.
He makes his own sweet life secure,
　And then—to crown all this—
Insults a God by thinking he'll
　Get everlasting bliss!

W. H. Davies

169.　THE NEWER VAINGLORY

Two men went up to pray; and one gave thanks,
　Not with himself—aloud,
With proclamation, calling on the ranks
　Of an attentive crowd.

"Thank God, I clap not my own humble breast,
　But other ruffians' backs,
Imputing crime—such is my tolerant haste—
　To any man that lacks.

"For I am tolerant, generous, keep no rules,
　And the age honors me.
Thank God, I am not as these rigid fools,
　Even as this Pharisee."

Alice Meynell

170. THE BETRAYAL

. . . And when I heard their voices on the stair,
Shrill as fox-bark above their crying hounds,
And heard the small thunder of their feet, and knew
One wall alone still lay
Between me and this stunted swarm,
I drew my last knife and I vowed to God
I should die first and not go down
Tied like a tame bear in their pygmy chains.

Then the lock shattered and they came
Flooding through once inviolate doors, and stood
World-deep around me in a crying ring that pressed
Nearer and nearer toward the brittle knife.
Then I,
Searching the wide, white ring to know
Who led them here and who betrayed
The soul's last citadel of pride,
Saw suddenly my own self standing there,
Pale-faced and simpering, unashamed,
Dwarf rope and key still dangling from my hand,
And then I knew the bitterness of Christ, and cried,
"Come take me, friends! Our little war is done."
—And broke the useless knife across my knee.

Josephine W. Johnson

171. EVIL IS HOMELESS

Evil has no home,
only evil has no home,
not even the home of demoniacal hell.
Hell is the home of souls lost in darkness,
even as heaven is the home of souls lost in light.
And like Persephone, or Attis

there are souls that are at home in both homes.
Not like grey Dante, colour-blind
to the scarlet and purple flowers at the doors of hell.

But evil
evil has no dwelling-place
the grey vulture, the grey hyaena, corpse-eaters
they dwell in the outskirt fringes of nowhere
where the grey twilight of evil sets in.

And men that sit in machines
among spinning wheels, in an apotheosis of wheels
sit in the grey mist of movement which moves not
and going which goes not
and doing which does not
and being which is not:
that is, they sit and are evil, in evil,
grey evil, which has no path, and shows neither light nor dark
and has no home, no home anywhere.

D. H. Lawrence

172.   TRAGEDY

This, of all fates, would be the saddest end;
That that heroic fever, with its cry
From Children unto Mother, "Here am I!"
Should lose the very faith it would defend;
That the high soul through passion should descend
To work the evil it had willed should die.
If it won so, would that be victory,
That tragic close? Oh, hearken, foe or friend!
Love, the magician, and the wizard Hate,
Though one be like white fire and one dark flame,
Work the same miracle, and all are wrought
Into the image that they contemplate.

None ever hated in the world but came
To every baseness of the foe he fought.

AE (George William Russell)

173. GOD'S EDUCATION

I saw him steal the light away
    That haunted in her eye:
It went so gently none could say
More than that it was there one day
    And missing by-and-by.

I watched her longer, and he stole
    Her lily tincts and rose;
All her young sprightliness of soul
Next fell beneath his cold control,
    And disappeared like those.

I asked: "Why do you serve her so?
    Do you, for some glad day,
Hoard these her sweets—?" He said, "O no,
They charm not me; I bid Time throw
    Them carelessly away."

Said I: "We call that cruelty—
    We, your poor mortal kind."
He mused. "The thought is new to me.
Forsooth, though I men's master be,
    Theirs is the teaching mind!"

Thomas Hardy

174. THE QUIET FLOWER

It will be with us always through our lives,
—This raw world, red and whistling in the light,

The shrill and accustomed doggerel of the days.
This we know now, and this we accept as ours,
Seeking no desert mount,
Scraping no sacred caves.

But there is the need of silence, deep, undying,
The need to be still, to turn and go
Back to a quiet acre in the hills, and there,
Small and alone beneath the arch of night,
Wash in a cold lake underneath the stars.

✠

Go now, before we are lost and shaken,
Flying with those who flee, pursuing with those who run.
Remember a dark and unchanging field,
Remember a quiet flower,
Unfound in red pastures of the sun.
   Turn back to this quiet acre in the night,
   And find the cold petals of that pristine star
   Which, alone and immaculate and white,
   Blossoms beyond the temporal hour.

Josephine W. Johnson

175. THE ANSWER

Then what is the answer?—Not to be deluded by dreams.
To know that great civilizations have broken down into violence,
            and their tyrants come, many times before.
When open violence appears, to avoid it with honor or choose the
            least ugly faction; these evils are essential.
To keep one's own integrity, to be merciful and uncorrupted and
            not wish for evil; and not be duped
By dreams of universal justice or happiness. These dreams will not
            be fulfilled.
To know this, and know that however ugly the parts appear the
            whole remains beautiful. A severed hand

Is an ugly thing, and man dissevered from the earth and stars and
        his history—for contemplation or in fact—
Often appears atrociously ugly. Integrity is wholeness, the greatest
                   beauty is
Organic wholeness, the wholeness of life and things, the divine
         beauty of the universe. Love that, not man
Apart from that, or else you will share man's pitiful confusions, or
        drown in despair when his days darken.

                   Robinson Jeffers

176. GOD'S THANKS TO JOB

From "A Masque of Reason"

I've had you on my mind a thousand years
To thank you someday for the way you helped me
Establish once for all the principle
There's no connection man can reason out
Between his just deserts and what he gets.
Virtue may fail and wickedness succeed.
'Twas a great demonstration we put on.
I should have spoken sooner had I found
The word I wanted. You would have supposed
One who in the beginning was the Word
Would be in a position to command it.
I have to wait for words like anyone.
Too long I've owed you this apology
For the apparently unmeaning sorrow
You were afflicted with in those old days.
But it was of the essence of the trial
You shouldn't understand it at the time.
It had to seem unmeaning to have meaning.
And it came out all right. I have no doubt
You realize by now the part you played
To stultify the Deuteronomist
And change the tenor of religious thought.
My thanks are to you for releasing me

From moral bondage to the human race.
The only free will there at first was man's,
Who could do good or evil as he chose.
I had no choice but I must follow him
With forfeits and rewards he understood—
Unless I liked to suffer loss of worship.
I had to prosper good and punish evil.
You changed all that. You set me free to reign.
You are the Emancipator of your God,
And as such I promote you to a saint.

Robert Frost

177.   GOD AND THE HOLY GHOST

There is no sinning against God, what does God care about sin!
But there is sinning against the Holy Ghost, since the Holy Ghost
is with us
in the flesh, is part of our consciousness.

The Holy Ghost is the deepest part of our own consciousness
wherein we know ourself for what we are
and know our dependence on the creative beyond.

So if we go counter to our own deepest consciousness
naturally we destroy the most essential self in us,
and once done, there is no remedy, no salvation for this,
nonentity is our portion.

D. H. Lawrence

178.   THE HANDS OF GOD

It is a fearful thing to fall into the hands of the living God.
But it is a much more fearful thing to fall out of them.

Did Lucifer fall through knowledge?
oh then, pity him, pity him that plunge!
Save me, O God, from falling into the ungodly knowledge
of myself as I am without God.
Let me never know, O God
let me never know what I am or should be
when I have fallen out of your hands, the hands of the living God.

That awful and sickening endless sinking, sinking
through the slow, corruptive levels of disintegrative knowledge
when the self has fallen from the hands of God
and sinks, seething and sinking, corrupt
and sinking still, in depth after depth of disintegrative consciousness
sinking in the endless undoing, the awful katabolism into the abyss!
even of the soul, fallen from the hands of God.

Save me from that, O God!
Let me never know myself apart from the living God!

D. H. Lawrence

179.   THE FEAR OF GOD

If you should rise from Nowhere up to Somewhere,
From being No one up to being Someone,
Be sure to keep repeating to yourself
You owe it to an arbitrary god
Whose mercy to you rather than to others
Won't bear too critical examination.
Stay unassuming. If for lack of license
To wear the uniform of who you are,
You should be tempted to make up for it
In a subordinating look or tone
Beware of coming too much to the surface,
And using for apparel what was meant
To be the curtain of the inmost soul.

Robert Frost

180.   A SMALL THOUGHT SPEAKS
FOR THE FLESH

Master, destined to be
Our immortality,
It is the flesh would speak,
Asking: What do you seek
Beyond these lives that run
Like lizards in the sun?

What shall you do with these,
Life's nerved complexities?
What will suffice for your
Last home, inheritor
Become the living ghost
Of life when we are lost?

Look how each flowing vein
Through flesh has charged all brain
From the quick animal heart
Has caused this thought to start
Endless in nerves that give
Us life that you may live.

Master, remote, alone,
Beyond all dying, done
With our mortality thus,
Oh, do not abandon us!
Think how our anguish must make
Some meaning for your sake.

                              Carleton Drewry

181.   THE MAN WITHOUT FAITH

A man without faith
Grows old before his years,

His world a wraith,
For whom the end nears
Like a winter mist
When the sun is cold
In the cold west.
His children about him
Are strangers, unknown.
The love that begot them
Cooled and gone.
If he get riches
They turn to rust,
And he can do nothing
With a handful of dust.
Life's miracle fails him,
Life's rapture, life's breath;
He has done with living,
He has forestalled death.

Richard Church

182.   EVEN IN THE DARKNESS

Even in the darkness, O seed,
Without light, or hope of the light,
Give praise to your God. Indeed,
Though mysteriously He smite
You down as you gather your strength,
Though He make of your life a thing
Without purpose or grace, and at length
Send upon you a quivering
Premature and inglorious death;
Yet give thanks to Him that He made,
Out of His will and His breath,
Out of His wisdom inlaid
With infinite mercy and pain,
A world wherein such things might be—
That through the disorder might strain

A tender shoot and a tree,
Sturdy buds and blossoms and fruit;
That of an inconsequent germ
Taking a haphazard root
Might be born a giant with firm
Body, and skill to defeat
The enmity of its kind,
The storm and the frost and the heat.
Even in the darkness, O blind
Seed, be not sunken and bound
With gloom when your own time is done,
As though life had never been found
To progress past the sod to the sun.

                              Helene Mullins

183.   INTERROGATIVE

Who can give answer to your questioning
Why the swift bird should fall with splintered wing?
Or the young child lie
Broken beneath the sky?
Why the first rose should know a blight?
Why in the city of the heart
There is a dreadful night?

Plato sought answers where the shadows run
In a cave pinioned by the sun;
The Stagirite
Teased the tall gates of reason night by night;
While stoics wrestling with inexorable fate
Chide death for being late.

Yet to this mystery
You hold the key.

A bare tree burgeoned on a hill,
Whose branches brushed the sky

High as your Christ was high;
Who, lithe limbs stark to the wood,
Beneath a thorn-thatched hood
Died and did not die—

But lives unendingly
In flesh of your humanity
To raise new calvaries
Over the sin parched sod,
Whereon new Christs shall hang
Whose bright veins run with God.

This is the simple answer
Even a child may understand
And cup in its small hand,
And yet a mystery still—
Since pain took glory on,
And sorrow bloomed on a hill.

Sister M. Therése

XIII   in this hour

"Auguries of self-annihilation loom"

184.   IN THIS HOUR

We saw the bare feet and the quiet hands sprawled on the street
stones.

We saw the passive hands turned with palms upward,
The blood on the ragged shirt and the eyes and the hair.
We saw the mouth that had cried out its creed, still believing:
Turn to him that shall smite you the other cheek also—
Split in the face, and the face bloody with nailed boots dragging
across it,
And over the body the iron hoofs driven,
Grinding bone deep in the frozen mud.
    What shall we say now? What shall we do now?
    The voices crying out over the thunder—
    Is the word broken forever? Is the branch a sword, and the cross
a sword?
    And the song written with swords hereafter?

All night we knelt down in frost by the body,
Under the cold stars waiting some answer out of the darkness,
Waiting to see the white fog of the spirit
Rise from the splintered mouth and ascend in the starlight.
Crying its answer.
    What did we kneel for? What did we ask for?
    How shall we face the terrible sound, the more terrible silence?—
This cry of the living-betrayed,
This stone on the mouths of the silent?

                                              Josephine W. Johnson

185.   THE UNKNOWN CITIZEN

(To JS/07/M/378 This Marble Monument Is Erected by the State)

He was found by the Bureau of Statistics to be
One against whom there was no official complaint,
And all the reports on his conduct agree
That, in the modern sense of an old-fashioned word, he was a saint,
For in everything he did he served the Greater Community.

Except for the War till the day he retired
He worked in a factory and never got fired,
But satisfied his empoyers, Fudge Motors, Inc.
Yet he wasn't a scab or odd in his views,
For his Union reports that he paid his dues,
(Our report on his Union shows it was sound)
And our Social Psychology workers found
That he was popular with his mates and liked a drink.
The Press are convinced that he bought a paper every day
And that his reactions to advertisements were normal in every way.
Policies taken out in his name prove that he was fully insured,
And his Health-card shows he was once in hospital but left it cured.
Both Producers Research and High-Grade Living declare
He was fully sensible to the advantages of the Instalment Plan
And had everything necessary to the Modern Man,
A phonograph, a radio, a car and a frigidaire.
Our Researchers into Public Opinion are content
That he held the proper opinions for the time of year;
When there was peace, he was for peace; when there was war, he
                                                                                    went.
He was married and added five children to the population,
Which our Eugenist says was the right number for a parent of his
                                                                              generation,
And our teachers report that he never interfered with their education.
Was he free? Was he happy? The question is absurd:
Had anything been wrong, we should certainly have heard.

W. H. Auden

186.   ADVICE TO A PROPHET

When you come, as you soon must, to the streets of our city,
Mad-eyed from stating the obvious,
Not proclaiming our fall but begging us
In God's name to have self-pity,

Spare us all word of the weapons, their force and range,
The long numbers that rocket the mind;

Our slow, unreckoning hearts will be left behind,
Unable to fear what is too strange.

Nor shall you scare us with talk of the death of the race.
How should we dream of this place without us?—
The sun mere fire, the leaves untroubled about us,
A stone look on the stone's face?

Speak of the world's own change. Though we cannot conceive
Of an undreamt thing, we know to our cost
How the dreamt cloud crumbles, the vines are blackened by frost,
How the view alters. We could believe,

If you told us so, that the white-tailed deer will slip
Into perfect shade, grown perfectly shy,
The lark avoid the reaches of our eye,
The jake-pine lose its knuckled grip

On the cold ledge, and every torrent burn
As Xanthus once, its gliding trout
Stunned in a twinkling. What should we be without
The dolphin's arc, the dove's return,

These things in which we have seen ourselves and spoken?
Ask us, prophet, how we shall call
Our natures forth when that live tongue is all
Dispelled, that glass obscured or broken

In which we have said the rose of our love and the clean
Horse of our courage, in which beheld
The singing locust of the soul unshelled,
And all we mean or wish to mean.

Ask us, ask us whether with the worldless rose
Our hearts shall fail us; come demanding
Whether there shall be lofty or long standing
When the bronze annals of the oak-tree close.

Richard Wilbur

187.   BABYLON

Babylon that was beautiful is Nothing now.
Once to the world it tolled a golden bell:
Belshazzar wore its blaze upon his brow;
Ruled; and to ruin fell.
Babylon—a blurred and blinded face of stone—
At dumb Oblivion bragged with trumpets blown;
Teemed, and while merchants throve and prophets dreamed,
Bowed before idols, and was overthrown.

Babylon the merciless, now a name of doom,
Built towers in Time, as we today, for whom
Auguries of self-annihilation loom.

Siegfried Sassoon

188.   SHINE, REPUBLIC

The quality of these trees, green height; of the sky, shining, of water,
                              a clear flow; of the rock, hardness
And reticence: each is noble in its quality. The love of freedom has
                    been the quality of Western man.

There is a stubborn torch that flames from Marathon to Concord,
                         its dangerous beauty binding three ages
Into one time; the waves of barbarism and civilization have eclipsed
                              but have never quenched it.

For the Greeks the love of beauty, for Rome of ruling, for the present
                    age the passionate love of discovery;
But in one noble passion we are one; and Washington, Luther,
                    Tacitus, Aeschylus, one kind of man.

And you, America, that passion made you. You were not born to
                    prosperity, you were born to love freedom.
You did not say "en masse," you said "independence." But we cannot
                    have all the luxuries and freedom also.

Freedom is poor and laborious; that torch is not safe but hungry, and
                     often requires blood for its fuel.
You will tame it against it burn too clearly, you will hood it like a
            kept hawk, you will perch it on the wrist of Caesar.

But keep the tradition, conserve the forms, the observances, keep the
             spot sore. Be great, carve deep your heel-marks.
The states of the next age will no doubt remember you, and edge
           their love of freedom with contempt of luxury.

                                Robinson Jeffers

189.   THE SECOND COMING

Turning and turning in the widening gyre
The falcon cannot hear the falconer;
Things fall apart; the centre cannot hold;
Mere anarchy is loosed upon the world,
The blood-dimmed tide is loosed, and everywhere
The ceremony of innocence is drowned;
The best lack all conviction, while the worst
Are full of passionate intensity.

Surely some revelation is at hand;
Surely the Second Coming is at hand.
The Second Coming! Hardly are those words out
When a vast image out of *Spiritus Mundi*
Troubles my sight; somewhere in sands of the desert
A shape with lion body and pitiless as the sun,
Is moving its slow thighs, while all about it
Reel shadows of the indignant desert birds.
The darkness drops again; but now I know
That twenty centuries of stony sleep
Were vexed to nightmare by a rocking cradle,
And what rough beast, its hour come round at last,
Slouches towards Bethlehem to be born?

                         William Butler Yeats

190.   POWERS AND TIMES
ARE NOT GODS

From "For the Time Being: A Christmas Oratorio"

These are stirring times for the editors of newspapers:
History is in the making; Mankind is on the march.
The longest aqueduct in the world is already
Under construction; the Committees on Fen-Drainage
And Soil-Conservation will issue very shortly
Their Joint Report; even the problems of Trade Cycles
And Spiralling Prices are regarded by the experts
As practically solved; and the recent restrictions
Upon aliens and free-thinking Jews are beginning
To have a salutary effect upon the public morale.
True, the Western seas are still infested with pirates,
And the rising power of the Barbarian in the North
Is giving some cause for uneasiness; but we are fully
Alive to these dangers; we are rapidly arming; and both
Will be taken care of in due course: then, united
In a sense of common advantage and common right,
Our great Empire shall be secure for a thousand years.
　　If we were never alone or always too busy,
Perhaps we might even believe what we know is not true:
But no one is taken in, at least not all of the time;
In our bath, or the subway, or the middle of the night,
We know very well we are not unlucky but evil,
That the dream of a Perfect State or No State at all,
To which we fly for refuge, is a part of our punishment.
　　Let us therefore be contrite but without anxiety,
For Powers and Times are not gods but mortal gifts from God;
Let us acknowledge our defeat but without despair
For all societies and epochs are transient details,
Transmitting an everlasting opportunity
That the Kingdom of Heaven may come, not in our present
And not in our future, but in the Fullness of Time.
Let us pray.

　　　　　　　　　　　　　　　　　　W. H. Auden

191.   PROTAGONIST

Astronomers predict his sun is dying;
when it grows cold the curious minor star
will toss the moons away, send planets flying
down vast ellipses where no seers are;
his rivers will be spilled, his dawns suspended,
his laughter lost among the empty spheres,
joy—which was never more than joy—all ended,
and tears which never were more than human tears.

But when in time will matter be again
so lightly swaddled as by living bands,
so brightly held as in his shallow hands,
so nearly known as in his breakable brain?
When will the joy deep in it speak and sing
again and grief of worlds be its own thing?

Edith Henrich

192.   THE FUNDAMENT IS SHIFTED

The call is for belief,
As once for doubt.
The old firm picture wavers
As if in water,
Like a thing off-centered.
The fundament is shifted by a hair's breadth;
What next we hear
May be the crack of doom—
Or be, instead,
Resurrection-horn blowing full A.

The physicist
In his high country of transparent landscape,
Who sees the mountains building, the chill growing
In the sun's flame-pit, dissolution snipping

Infinitesimal threads as grain flees grain
Under the beat of the wind and the rain and the sea—
He now, earth's cautious man,
Hazards a blinding guess that he is seeing
—Sprinkled apart, here, there, in the erst-failing cosmos—
Sun-creation raging in its might,
Rising to replace.
And others still,
Outrunning reach of dim-lit eye, make probe
Of modes of being more intense, and powers
Inchoate, dark, glimpsed to be lost again.

Men quail before such newness.
If less hinged upon it,
We were less bleak-minded;
Would dare to trust our weight
On what is weightless,
And, like the astronaut,
With open eye
Step out on empty space as on a shelf,
Above the plane of falling.

And not fall.

                                        Abbie Huston Evans

XIV VISION, THE INTERIOR LIFE

"In certain minds the strength wells
In richness from subterranean springs"

193.   BUT GOD'S OWN DESCENT

But God's own descent
Into flesh was meant
As a demonstration
That the supreme merit
Lay in risking spirit
In transubstantiation.
Spirit enters flesh
And for all it's worth
Changes into earth
In birth after birth
Ever fresh and fresh.
We may take the view
That its derring-do
Thought of in the large
Is one mighty charge
On our human part
Of the soul's ethereal
Into the material.

Robert Frost

194.   IN THE BEGINNING

In the beginning was the three-pointed star,
One smile of light across the empty face;
One bough of bone across the rooting air,
The substance forked that marrowed the first sun;
And, burning ciphers on the round of space,
Heaven and hell mixed as they spun.

In the beginning was the pale signature,
Three-syllabled and starry as the smile;
And after came the imprints on the water,
Stamp of the minted face upon the moon;
The blood that touched the crosstree and the grail
Touched the first cloud and left a sign.

In the beginning was the mounting fire
That set alight the weathers from a spark,
A three-eyed, red-eyed spark, blunt as a flower;
Life rose and spouted from the rolling seas,
Burst in the roots, pumped from the earth and rock
The secret oils that drive the grass.

In the beginning was the word, the word
That from the solid bases of the light
Abstracted all the letters of the void;
And from the cloudy bases of the breath
The word flowed up, translating to the heart
First characters of birth and death.

In the beginning was the secret brain.
The brain was celled and soldered in the thought
Before the pitch was forking to a sun;
Before the veins were shaking in their sieve,
Blood shot and scattered to the winds of light
The ribbed original of love.

Dylan Thomas

195.   THE MOMENT OF VISION

The moment of vision will come when it will,
The gift of the gods, the unshakable
Unbreakable
Subtle intuitive stewardship, and still
That matchless satisfaction of the maker.

To read the spirit was all my care and is,
To lose life to find hope,
To destroy in the heady grope
For new worlds upon an old's effacement,
Through the breach of evil the breath of grace.

Those men who fight for the spirit have my love,
Fierce young poets tearing their hearts out,
Strong for many materialistic bouts,
Destroyers who put on creation like a glove,
Wear grace from their despair: the wrenched fist.

The worthy one who did a worthier thing
Than all the worthies did—he kept that hid;
Him whom another age heard not,
But now my surest music of the word,
Earth-thrown singer, who burnt his bridges.

Richard Eberhart

196.   THE BEATIFIC VISION

Through what fierce incarnations, furled
    In fire and darkness, did I go,
Ere I was worthy in the world
    To see a dandelion grow?

Well, if in any woes or wars
    I bought my naked right to be,
Grew worthy of the grass, nor gave
    The wren, my brother, shame for me.

But what shall God not ask of him
    In the last time when all is told,
Who saw her stand beside the hearth,
    The firelight garbing her in gold?

G. K. Chesterton

197.   LIGHT

Now with drums
Light comes.
It knocks

Upon no door;
From no dim pane
It stirs the dust
Or sweeps the skein
That is the spider's airy fane.
It turns no locks.
It has no language to implore
The just,
No thunder to awake
The sluggard and the rake.
It wields no instrument of doom
To raise the sombre siege of gloom;
It spins no stratagems with mirth.
But to the wide, clear-windowed room
It is rebirth.

Herman Hagedorn

198. THE INCOMPARABLE LIGHT

The light beyond compare is the light I saw.
I saw it on the mountain tops, the light
Beyond compare. I saw it in childhood too.
I glimpsed it in the turbulence of growing up.
I saw it in the meshes of meaning of women.
I saw it in political action, and I saw
The light beyond compare in sundry deaths.

Elusive element, final mystery,
The light beyond compare has been my visitant,
Some sort of angel sometimes at my shoulder,
A beckoning guide, elusive nevertheless,
Under the mind where currents of being are running.
It is this strange light I come back to,
Agent of truth, protean, a radical of time.

The light beyond compare is my meaning,
It is the secret source of my beginning,

Issuance of uniqueness, signal upon suffering,
It is the wordless bond of all endings,
It is the subtle flash that tells our song,
Inescapable brotherhood of the living,
Our mystery of time, the only hopeful light.

                                                   Richard Eberhart

199.   THE WORK OF HAPPINESS

I thought of happiness, how it is woven
Out of the silence in the empty house each day
And how it is not sudden and it is not given
But is creation itself like the growth of a tree.
No one has seen it happen, but inside the bark
Another circle is growing in the expanding ring.
No one has heard the root go deeper in the dark,
But the tree is lifted by this inward work
And its plumes shine, and its leaves are glittering.

So happiness is woven out of the peace of hours
And strikes its roots deep in the house alone:
The old chest in the corner, cool waxed floors,
White curtains softly and continually blown
As the free air moves quietly about the room;
A shelf of books, a table, and the white-washed wall—
These are the dear familiar gods of home,
And here the work of faith can best be done,
The growing tree is green and musical.

For what is happiness but growth in peace,
The timeless sense of time when furniture
Has stood a life's span in a single place,
And as the air moves, so the old dreams stir
The shining leaves of present happiness.
No one has heard thought or listened to a mind,
But where people have lived in inwardness

The air is charged with blessing and does bless;
Windows look out on mountains and the walls are kind.

May Sarton

200. ON THE BUILDING OF SPRINGFIELD

Let not our town be large, remembering
That little Athens was the Muses' home,
That Oxford rules the heart of London still,
That Florence gave the Renaissance to Rome.

Record it for the grandson of your son—
A city is not builded in a day:
Our little town cannot complete her soul
Till countless generations pass away.

Now let each child be joined as to a church
To her perpetual hopes, each man ordained:
Let every street be made a reverent aisle
Where Music grows and Beauty is unchained.

Let Science and Machinery and Trade
Be slaves of her, and make her all in all,
Building against our blatant, restless time
An unseen, skilful, medieval wall.

Let every citizen be rich toward God.
Let Christ the beggar, teach divinity.
Let no man rule who holds his money dear.
Let this, our city, be our luxury.

We should build parks that students from afar
Would choose to starve in, rather than go home,
Fair little squares, with Phidian ornament,
Food for the spirit, milk and honeycomb.

Songs shall be sung by us in that good day,
Songs we have written, blood within the rhyme
Beating, as when Old England still was glad,—
The purple, rich Elizabethan time.

☒

Say, is my prophecy too fair and far?
I only know, unless her faith be high,
The soul of this, our Nineveh, is doomed,
Our little Babylon will surely die.

Some city on the breast of Illinois
No wiser and no better at the start
By faith shall rise redeemed, by faith shall rise
Bearing the western glory in her heart.

The genius of the Maple, Elm and Oak,
The secret hidden in each grain of corn,
The glory that the prairie angels sing
At night when sons of Life and Love are born,

Born but to struggle, squalid and alone,
Broken and wandering in their early years.
When will they make our dusty streets their goal,
Within our attics hide their sacred tears?

When will they start our vulgar blood athrill
With living language, words that set us free?
When will they make a path of beauty clear
Between our riches and our liberty?

We must have many Lincoln-hearted men.
A city is not builded in a day.
And they must do their work, and come and go,
While countless generations pass away.

                                        Vachel Lindsay

201.   FEMINA CONTRA MUNDUM

The sun was black with judgment, and the moon
   Blood: but between
I saw a man stand, saying, 'To me at least
   The grass is green.

'There was no star that I forgot to fear
   With love and wonder.
The birds have loved me;' but no answer came—
   Only the thunder.

Once more the man stood, saying, 'A cottage door,
   Wherethrough I gazed
That instant as I turned—yea, I am vile;
   Yet my eyes blazed.

'For I had weighed the mountains in a balance,
   And the skies in a scale,
I come to sell the stars—old lamps for new—
   Old stars for sale.'

Then a calm voice fell all the thunder through,
   A tone less rough:
'Thou hast begun to love one of my works
   Almost enough.'

G. K. Chesterton

202.   THE PLEA

If ever at Saint Peter's gate
   I call "Who's there within?"
And he, the bailey, bids me wait
   The audit of my sin,
     I'll make no plea, in my defence,
     Of charity or continence.

I know too well how meagre still
  Has been my love's excess,
What poor infirmity of will
  My chronicles confess,
    To ask that these should mitigate
    The resolution of my fate.

But I will take a garland green
  Of quiet English hours,
"Of such," I'll say, "good saint, has been
  My learning." And the flowers
    Of Peter's Paradise will shine
    On these, and make those gardens mine.

John Drinkwater

203. RECONCILIATION

I begin through the grass once again to be bound to the Lord;
I can see, through a face that has faded, the face full of rest
Of the earth, of the mother, my heart with her heart in accord,
As I lie 'mid the cool green tresses that mantle her breast
I begin with the grass once again to be bound to the Lord.

By the hand of a child I am led to the throne of the King
For a touch that now fevers me not is forgotten and far,
And His infinite sceptered hands that sway us can bring
Me in dreams from the laugh of a child to the song of a star.
On the laugh of a child I am borne to the joy of the King.

AE (George William Russell)

204. THE RICH INTERIOR LIFE

In certain minds the strength wells
In richness from subterranean springs,

As if music were forever
Growing out of pregnant cells.

It is as if, in deep desire
The mind did not quite wish to know
Itself, withheld its sale,
Sensing its own demise in hire,

And would, in its pastures of increase,
Express the far ease of its spring
Where, in hallowed shade of long day
It wells as it would never cease.

In certain minds there is a pure grace
As through harsh rocks upwelling.
There is the strength of humanity;
There, the truth beyond the telling.

There are broad and open fields of ease
Where the waters go in rich mornings.
The true heart plays at ease there,
In the music of those mornings.

Richard Eberhart

205.   NEW YEAR WISHES

May these delights be yours in the new year:
Above the pressure of chaotic fear,
Below the pressure of chaotic love—
An inward order set below, above.
Anxiety and passion both are sins
But pure creation is where joy begins.
But pure creation is where springs delight
Winged at birth and fully armed for flight,
The phoenix of the mind, who from despair,
Leaps to the radiant margins of the air:

These be your joys by the new year bestowed,
To make your raiment of celestial cloud.

Run down the forest-gamut of the notes to seize
(But never catch him) Mozart in the trees,
The prodigal, the flute-bird tossing songs
Into the timeless leaves in shining throngs.

To keep the book marked to the Rousseau-page
Where lies The Sleeping Gipsy's entranced image,
His lute beside him while the awed lion creeps
To sniff the marble quiet of this man who sleeps.

To keep another open so that Sabrina's pool
May yield her up when the wild heart is cool,
And from the airy caverns of her wave,
That innocent, Imagination, rise and save.

This, the immaculate and ordered joy
Of pure creation, no trouble can destroy.
It is as nothing in the world can be
Absolved from change, the only certainty,
"The bracelet of bright hair about the bone"
That makes a living lover of the skeleton,
The timeless life, the fiery star that swings
In an eternal night and there forever sings.

May Sarton

206.   ADDRESS TO MY SOUL

My soul, be not disturbed
By planetary war;
Remain securely orbed
In this contracted star.

Fear not, pathetic flame;
Your sustenance is doubt:

Glassed in translucent dream
They cannot snuff you out.

Wear water, or a mask
Of unapparent cloud;
Be brave and never ask
A more defunctive shroud.

The universal points
Are shrunk into a flower;
Between its delicate joints
Chaos keeps no power.

The pure integral form,
Austere and silver-dark,
Is balanced on the storm
In its predestined arc.

Small as a sphere of rain
It slides along the groove
Whose path is furrowed plain
Among the suns that move.

The shapes of April buds
Outlive the phantom year:
Upon the void at odds
The dewdrop falls severe.

Five-petalled flame, be cold:
Be firm, dissolving star:
Accept the stricter mould
That makes you singular.

Elinor Wylie

207.   ST. FRANCIS AND THE CLOUD

". . . forget all creatures that ever God made . . . with a seemly
recklessness take no heed of them. . . . as this *cloud of unknowing*

is betwixt thee and thy God, so put a *cloud of forgetting* betwixt thee
and all creatures."

> With such unseemly caution have I taken heed
> That now, if I stand, if I run, if I lie down,
> Awake in my speaking, asleep in my dreaming prayers
> I must remember.
>
> The birds bend wing as I kneel.
>
> In my sleep the lamb in his aureole of wool,
> The lion in the halo of his mane
> Ramble together like God's works, my dream.
>
> How can I not remember when I run
> The rapid wind, the spaces of His voice;
> The rock, His depths of silence, when I stand;
> When I break bread, the heavens of His crumbs?
>
> All things remind me:
> All bones of angels,
> All fires of grass,
> All ashes of the sun.
>
> How can I forget the rays of light in the light
> Or the roots in the darkness, or myself
> In the dust, in the air, their mingling?
>
> I forget nothing. I am unseemly.
>
> All these distractions in the loves of God,
> The action of these dreams between His works
> Amuse God's lovers in their love of God.
>
> But how shall I put on the innocent cloud
> And love Him not in work, His works of love,
> And all unknowing, love only His being?

I am not worthy. All things remind me:
All tombs of shells,
All clay of birth,
All sorrows of green vines.

Most heedful of His works, I am least use,
Most careful of His loves, I am most cold,
Most knowing of His creatures, I am lost.

And yet I am unknowing of despair.

All things remind me:
All is generous.

The beast that knows a little less than I
Clothes in his little mist my naked care
And being hid in the more reckless bird
The bird in the most seemly recklessness
Is held, is hidden in the crumb of bread

And all things clouding, sky by deeper sky,
Brother by worthier brother I may come
To all unknowing that is loving God.

Marie De L. Welch

208.   FOUNDATION OF FAITH

Further than this we may not know,
   Diviners though we be,
That from the seed warmed by the snow
   The bud bursts to the tree,
And thence the leaves in showering gold
Flutter, and seek again the mould.

The hazels slip their hods, the grain
   Is garnered, and the dews

Wash earth, and to the clouds again
    Are gathered; and the news
Of one star counted more or less
Makes all our wisdom, idleness.

Peace, then; beyond the time we are
    Dwells the eternal mind,
That, though we seek it here and far
    And seeking do not find,
Holds all the tides and seasons thus,
And shall by law deliver us.

                  John Drinkwater

209.   COMING HOME

You are coming home at night:
You pass from light to light,
Walking around the block,
And your shadow swings to the right
The way the second hand
Goes round a modern clock,
And other shadows, bound
To your footsteps, climb the walls,
Or jerk along the pavement,
And some contract and darken,
Others lengthen and fade.

The lights are various loves
By whom you find your way,
By whom you see and move:
They lend you guidance, they
Enable you to find
Not only house and door,
And wall and window-blind,
But something less and more,
Your image, multiplied,

Cast for your gaze, and thrown
Distorted, but your own.

And what you need the most,
O walker in the night,
Is to continue, sure
The self is really there,
The self is always right,
And neither caricature,
Nor unavailing ghost.

And if a light is broken,
If one of them goes out,
As well they may, of course,
And substance takes from shadow
Its absolute divorce,
Be reassured, in darkness,
The self is never lost.

Rolfe Humphries

210. THIS CORRUPTIBLE

The Body, long oppressed
And pierced, then prayed for rest
(Being but apprenticed to the other Powers);
And kneeling in that place
Implored the thrust of grace
Which makes the dust lie level with the flowers.

Then did that fellowship
Of three, the Body strip;
Beheld his wounds, and none among them mortal;
The Mind severe and cool;
The Heart still half a fool;
The fine-spun Soul, a beam of sun can startle.

These three, a thousand years
Had made adventurers
Amid all villainies the earth can offer,
Applied them to resolve
From the universal gulph
What pangs the poor material flesh may suffer.

"This is a pretty pass;
To hear the growing grass
Complain; the clay cry out to be translated;
Will not this grosser stuff
Receive reward enough
If stabled after labouring, and baited?"

Thus spoke the Mind in scorn:
The Heart, which had outworn
The Body, and was weary of its fashion,
Preferring to be dressed
In skin of bird or beast,
Replied more softly, in a feigned compassion.

"Anatomy most strange
Crying to chop and change;
Inferior copy of a higher image;
While I, the noblest guest,
Sick of your second-best
Sigh for embroidered archangelic plumage:

"For shame, thou fustian cloak!"
And then the Spirit spoke:
Within the void it swung securely tethered
By strings composed of cloud;
It spoke both low and loud
Above a storm no lesser star had weathered.

"O lodging for the night!
O house of my delight!

O lovely hovel builded for my pleasure!
Dear tenement of clay
Endure another day
As coffin fitted to my measure.

"Take Heart, and call to Mind
Although we are unkind;
Although we steal your shelter, strength, and clothing;
'Tis you who shall escape
In some enchanting shape
Or be dissolved to elemental nothing.

"You, the unlucky slave,
Are the lily on the grave;
The wave that runs above the bones a-whitening;
You are the new-mown grass;
And the wheaten bread of the Mass;
And the fabric of the rain, and the lightning.

"If one of us elect
To leave the poor suspect
Imperfect bosom of the earth our parent;
And from the world aveil
The Spirit of the Heart
Upon a further and essential errand;

"His chain he cannot slough
Nor cast his substance off;
He bears himself upon his flying shoulder;
The Heart, infirm and dull;
The Mind, in any skull;
And captive still, and wearier and colder.

" 'Tis you who are the ghost,
Disintegrated, lost;
The burden shed; the dead who need not bear it;
O grain of God in power,

Endure another hour!
It is but for an hour," said the Spirit.

Elinor Wylie

211.   STRANGENESS OF HEART

When I have lost the power to feel the pang
Which first I felt in childhood when I woke
And heard the unheeding garden bird who sang
Strangeness of heart for me while morning broke;
Or when in latening twilight sure with spring,
Pausing on homeward paths along the wood,
No sadness thrills my thought while thrushes sing,
And I'm no more the listening child who stood
So many sunsets past and could not say
What wandering voices called from far away:
    When I have lost those simple spells that stirred
    My being with an untranslated song,
    Let me go home for ever; I shall have heard
    Death; I shall know that I have lived too long.

Siegfried Sassoon

212.   ARE YOU BORN?

A child riding the stormy mane of noon
Sang to me past the cloud of the world:
Are you born? Are you born?
The form of this hope is the law of all things,
Our foaming sun is the toy of that force.
—Touch us alive, developing light! Today,
Revealed over the mountains, every living eyes.

Child of the possible, who rides the hour
Of dream and process, lit by every fire.
Glittering blood of song, a man who changed

And hardly changed, only flickered, letting pass
A glint of time, showers of human meanings
Flashing upon us all: his story and his song.
The song of a child; the song of the cloud of the world,
Born, born, born. Cloud become real, and change,
The starry form of love.

                                                        Muriel Rukeyser

213.   REMEMBER THE SOURCE

          Let me pour upon the mind
          Strong fevers of the blood,
          Let the blood that came from Adam
          Put on the scholar's cap and hood,

          Let it tell the distance and the dell,
          Let it stretch reasonable frames
          Saying all dark vessels sailing well
          Are inventions whence dark music came,

          Let the imagination leaping
          Leap to sunward images
          And hold the universe commingled,
          Controlled by the blood's rages,

          That no man think fair dreams
          Were free, or forced, but true
          To the fate of God's own charity,
          Where all our hopes are new.

          Spirit, be bright to build!
          Blood be red in the dark flow.
          Every work of noble mind
          Is a noble work of God.

                                        Richard Eberhart

214.   APOCALYPSE

God is coming!
Hear the wind of his Spirit
Rushing through the upper reaches of the mind.
Bolt no door, turn no key:
Roof will be shaken from floor.
Hear the crash of wall,
The fall of tree,
And the sound of towers that smash.
Never came such a gale on earth,
Fanning spark to flame.
Nothing is safe but flung seed,
Spun spray, birds' wings
And flower petals that weigh
Nothing at all.
Nothing is safe but what flies,
But what sings;
Nothing dies but what is strong.
Prepare for the wheels of the wind
Racing through the upper air!
The atmosphere quivers and shakes,
The world quakes: God is coming.
His Holy Spirit is here!

Edith Lovejoy Pierce

215.   CLOSING CADENCE

Companion me,
Infused through every mood,
Transforming peace,
Genius of inwardhood:

Teach me to ask
For no precarious bliss
But to observe
Time's covenant of grace

As I allow
Perfecting of your will,
Deaf to what claims
Distract the interval

Between such hints
As insight shone before
And further light
Replenishing my share

On its return.
As when the music draws,
In a great fugue,
To its compelling close,

The steady flow
Of the firm organ-point
Marshals the notes
In luminous restraint

—After the clash
Of contrapuntal stress
Has given way
To clear harmoniousness,

When the whole web
Of interwoven tone
Moves to converge
In ultimate unison—

So let your cool,
Unhurried requiem
Guide my close,
Attend me out of time.

                              John Moffit

XV MORTALITY

"Think, Man of Flesh, and be not proud"

216.   DIRGE WITHOUT MUSIC

I am not resigned to the shutting away of loving hearts in the hard
                ground.
So it is, and so it will be, for so it has been, time out of mind:
Into the darkness they go, the wise and the lovely.
   Crowned
With lilies and laurel they go: but I am not resigned.

Lovers and thinkers, into the earth with you.
Be one with the dull, the indiscriminate dust.
A fragment of what you felt, of what you knew,
A formula, a phrase remains,—but the best is lost.

The answers quick and keen, the honest look, the laughter, the love,—
They are gone. They are gone to feed the roses.
   Elegant and curled
Is the blossom. Fragrant is the blossom. I know.
   But I do not approve.
More precious was the light in your eyes than all the roses of the
                world.

Down, down, down into the darkness of the grave
Gently they go, the beautiful, the tender, the kind;
Quietly they go, the intelligent, the witty, the brave.
I know. But I do not approve. And I am not resigned.

Edna St. Vincent Millay

217.   DEATH CAROL
"When Lilacs Last in the Door-yard Bloom'd"

Come, lovely and soothing Death,
Undulate round the world, serenely arriving, arriving,
In the day, in the night, to all, to each,
Sooner or later, delicate Death.

Prais'd be the fathomless universe,
For life and joy, and for objects and knowledge curious;
And for love, sweet love—But praise! praise! praise!
For the sure-enwinding arms of cool-enfolding Death.

Dark Mother, always gliding near, with soft feet,
Have none chanted for thee a chant of fullest welcome?
Then I chant it for thee—I glorify thee above all;
I bring thee a song that when thou must indeed come, come
                                                    unfalteringly.

Approach, strong Deliveress!
When it is so—when thou hast taken them, I joyously sing the dead,
Lost in the loving, floating ocean of thee,
Laved in the flood of thy bliss, O Death.

From me to thee glad serenades,
Dances for thee I propose, saluting thee—adornments and feastings
                                                    for thee;
And the sights of the open landscape, and the high-spread sky, are
                                                    fitting,
And life and the fields, and the huge and thoughtful night.

The night, in silence, under many a star;
The ocean shore, and the husky whispering wave, whose voice I
                                                    know;
And the soul turning to thee, O vast and well-veil'd Death,
And the body gratefully nestling close to thee.

Over the tree-tops I float thee a song!
Over the rising and sinking waves—over the myriad fields, and the
                                                    prairies wide;
Over the dense-pack'd cities all, and the teeming wharves and ways,
I float this carol with joy, with joy to thee, O Death!

                                                    Walt Whitman

218.   A SONG IN HUMILITY

Let me no more despise
Such creatures as comprise
Earth's lowliest, the least
Of life below the beast
Man binds, the bird brought down:

The ant on crowded crown
Of clay, the evening gnat:
Brief butterfly who sat
On such a tiny twig
Her body blossomed big,
Wings balanced like a blade;
The worm split by my spade;
The midge, the mindless fly;
All things that live and die:

All quick things that are caught,
All creatures come to naught
In parallel of these
Life's littler entities.

Nothing is old or new
In doing what all do,
So vast a thing as die.
None is more great than I,
And nothing is too small
To thus accomplish all.

Carleton Drewry

219.   SPEED

Think, Man of Flesh, and be not proud
    That you can fly so fast:
The little Worms can creep, creep, creep,

And catch you up at last—
Catch up with you at last.

Though you outfly the swiftest bird,
And laugh as you go past,
Think how the Worm comes, creep, creep, creep,
To catch you up at last—
Catch up with you at last.

W. H. Davies

220. THE MORNING AFTER DEATH

The bustle in a house
The morning after death
Is solemnest of industries
Enacted upon earth,—

The sweeping up the heart,
And putting love away
We shall not want to use again
Until eternity.

Emily Dickinson

221. THE FOUR AGES OF MAN

He with body waged a fight,
But body won; it walks upright.

Then he struggled with the heart;
Innocence and peace depart.

Then he struggled with the mind;
His proud heart he left behind.

Now his wars on God begin;
At stroke of midnight God shall win.
                              William Butler Yeats

222.   THE OVERTAKELESSNESS OF THOSE

The overtakelessness of those
Who have accomplished death,
Majestic is to me beyond
The majesties of Earth.

The soul her "not at Home"
Inscribes upon the flesh,
And takes her fair aerial gait
Beyond the hope of touch.
                              Emily Dickinson

223.   I SAID TO THE LEAF

Searching the earth, with exile worn,
I turned to a tree and a leaf that was torn.

Brother, I said to the leaf one day,
We must have come a long, long way

From earth to keep, each, an estate
Thus singularly separate,

Yet thus inseparately one:
Both thrust up blindly at the sun.

Or if earth aimed us at a star,
She has long forgotten where we are.

Brother, at length to the leaf I said,
We are the disinherited,

We are expatriates between
Earth that uplifts and skies that lean.

And to what land do we belong?
We are between the source and the song.

Some broken gesture leaves us now
Each on the end of a rotting bough

Whose radius was from the root.
Though life sings through us we are mute.

Though we were laved with light from birth
We are dark inside as the heart of earth.

And this, I think, is our gravest grief,
I said at last, I said to the leaf.

                              Carleton Drewry

224. BECAUSE I COULD NOT STOP
FOR DEATH

Because I could not stop for Death,
He kindly stopped for me;
The carriage held but just ourselves
And immortality.

We slowly drove, he knew no haste,
And I had put away
My labor, and my leisure too,
For his civility.

We passed the school where children played
At wrestling in a ring;
We passed the fields of gazing grain,
We passed the setting sun.

We paused before a house that seemed
A swelling of the ground;
The roof was scarcely visible,
The cornice but a mound.

Since then 'tis centuries; but each
Feels shorter than the day
I first surmised the horses' heads
Were toward eternity.

                              Emily Dickinson

225.   TESTAMENT

There are too many poems with the word
Death, death, death, tolling among the rhyme.
Let us remember death, a soaring bird
Whose wing will shadow all of us in time.

Let us remember death, an accident
Of darkness fallen far away and near.
But, being mortal, be most eloquent
Of daylight and the moment now and here.

Not to the name of death over and over,
But the prouder name of life, is poetry sworn.
The living man has words that rediscover
Even the dust from whence the man was born,

And words that may be water, food, and fire,
Of love and pity and perfection wrought,
Or swords or roses, as we may require,
Or sudden towers for the climbing thought.

Out of the beating heart the words that beat
Sing of the fountain that is never spent.

Let us remember life, the salt, the sweet,
And make of that our tireless testament.

John Holmes

226.   AUTUMNAL

Face it—you must—and do not turn away
From this bright day,
Intolerably glorious and bright,
Red-gold and blue by day, white-gold and blue by night.

Face it, and doing so,
Be wise enough to know
It is Death you face, it is Death whose colors burn
Gold, bronze, vermilion in the season's turn.

But Death with honor, gay
In pomp and fine array,
In glory and pride, spectacular and bright,
Gathering, giving, light.

A pure translation, whose impermanence
Informs the watching sense
Not with despair, but memory and praise
Of the three other seasons' perfect days.

Not only all that lives, but all that dies
Is holy, having lived, and testifies
To bravery in season, spirit, man.
Face it. You must. You can.

Rolfe Humphries

227.   THE ABSENT

They are not here. And we, we are the Others
Who walk by ourselves unquestioned in the sun

Which shines for us and only for us.
For They are not here.
And are made known to us in this great absence
That lies upon us and is between us
Since They are not here.
Now, in this kingdom of summer idleness
Where slowly we the sun-tranced multitudes dream and wander
In deep oblivion of brightness
And breathe ourselves out, out into the air—
It is absence that receives us;
We do not touch, our souls go out in the absence
That lies between us and is about us.
For we are the Others,
And so we sorrow for Those that are not with us,
Not knowing we sorrow or that this is our sorrow,
Since it is long past thought or memory or device of mourning,
Sorrow for loss of that which we never possessed,
The unknown, the nameless,
The ever-present that in their absence are with us
(With us the inheritors, the usurpers claiming
The sun and the kingdom of the sun) that sorrow
And loneliness might bring a blessing upon us.

Edwin Muir

228.   AFTER SUNSET

I have an understanding with the hills
At evening when the slanted radiance fills
Their hollows, and the great winds let them be,
And they are quiet and look down at me.
Oh, then I see the patience in their eyes
Out of the centuries that made them wise.
They lend me hoarded memory and I learn
Their thoughts of granite and their whims of fern,
And why a dream of forests must endure

Though every tree be slain: and how the pure,
Invisible beauty has a word so brief
A flower can say it or a shaken leaf,
But few may ever snare it in a song,
Though for the quest a life is not too long.
When the blue hills grow tender, when they pull
The twilight close with gesture beautiful,
And shadows are their garments, and the air
Deepens, and the wild verry is at prayer,—
Their arms are strong around me; and I know
That somehow I shall follow when you go
To the still land beyond the evening star,
Where everlasting hills and valleys are:
And silence may not hurt us any more,
And terror shall be past, and grief, and war.

                                        Grace Hazard Conkling

229.   ACCEPTANCE

When the spent sun throws up its rays on cloud
And goes down burning into the gulf below,
No voice in nature is heard to cry aloud
At what has happened. Birds, at least, must know
It is the change to darkness in the sky.
Murmuring something quiet in her breast,
One bird begins to close a faded eye;
Or overtaken too far from his nest,
Hurrying low above the grove, some waif
Swoops just in time to his remembered tree.
At most he thinks or twitters softly, 'Safe!
Now let the night be dark for all of me.
Let the night be too dark for me to see
Into the future. Let what will be, be.'

                                        Robert Frost

230. ALL-SOULS' DAY

Close-wrapped in living thought I stand
Where death and daybreak divide the land—
Death and daybreak on either hand
For exit and for entry;
While shapes like wind-blown shadows pass,
Lost and lamenting, 'Alas, alas,
This body is only shrivelling grass,
And the soul a starlit sentry
Who guards, and as he comes and goes,
Points now to daybreak's charnel close
Leans with regretless warning'. . . .
   I hear them thus—O thus I hear
   My doomed companions crowding near,
   Until my faith, absolved from fear,
   Sings out into the morning,
   And tells them how we travel far,
   From life to life, from star to star;
   Exult, unknowing what we are;
   And quell the obscene derision
   Of demon-haunters in our heart
   Who work for worms and have no part
   In Thee, O ultimate power, who art
   Our victory and our vision.

Siegfried Sassoon

XVI TRANSCENDENCE

"Men dance on deathless feet"

231.   MOHINI CHATTERJEE

I asked if I should pray,
But the Brahmin said,
'Pray for nothing, say
Every night in bed,
"I have been a king,
I have been a slave,
Nor is there anything,
Fool, rascal, knave,
That I have not been,
And yet upon my breast
A myriad heads have lain." '

That he might set at rest
A boy's turbulent days
Mohini Chatterjee
Spoke these, or words like these.
I add in commentary,
'Old lovers yet may have
All that time denied—
Grave is heaped on grave
That they be satisfied—
Over the blackened earth
The old troops parade,
Birth is heaped on birth
That such cannonade
May thunder time away,
Birth-hour and death-hour meet,
Or, as great sages say,
Men dance on deathless feet.'

William Butler Yeats

232.   A CREED

I hold that when a person dies
His soul returns again to earth;

Arrayed in some new flesh-disguise
  Another mother gives him birth.
With sturdier limbs and brighter brain
The old soul takes the road again.

Such is my own belief and trust;
  This hand, this hand that holds the pen,
Has many a hundred times been dust
  And turned, as dust, to dust again;
These eyes of mine have blinked and shone
In Thebes, in Troy, in Babylon.

All that I rightly think or do,
  Or make, or spoil, or bless, or blast,
Is curse or blessing justly due
  For sloth or effort in the past.
My life's a statement of the sum
Of vice indulged, or overcome.

I know that in my lives to be
  My sorry heart will ache or burn,
And worship, unavailingly,
  The woman whom I used to spurn,
And shake to see another have
The love I spurned, the love she gave.

And I shall know, in angry words,
  In gibes, and mocks, and many a tear,
A carrion flock of homing-birds,
  The gibes and scorns I uttered here.
The brave word that I failed to speak
Will brand me dastard on the cheek.

And as I wander on the roads
  I shall be helped and healed and blessed;
Dear words shall cheer and be as goads
  To urge to heights before unguessed.

My road shall be the road I made;
All that I gave shall be repaid.

So shall I fight, so shall I tread,
   In this long war beneath the stars;
So shall a glory wreathe my head,
   So shall I faint and show the scars,
Until this case, this clogging mould,
Be smithied all to kingly gold.

John Masefield

233.   MAN-TEST

When in the dim beginning of the years,
God mixed in man the raptures and the tears
And scattered through his brain the starry stuff,
He said, "Behold! Yet this is not enough,
For I must test his spirit to make sure
That he can dare the Vision and endure.

"I will withdraw my Face,
Veil me in shadow for a certain space,
Leaving behind Me only a broken clue—
A crevice where the glory glimmers through,
Some whisper from the sky,
Some footprint in the road to track Me by.

"I will leave man to make the fateful guess,
Will leave him torn between the No and Yes,
Leave him unresting till he rests in Me,
Drawn upward by the choice that makes him free—
Leave him in tragic loneliness to choose,
With all in life to win or all to lose."

Edwin Markham

234.   A NOISELESS PATIENT SPIDER

A noiseless patient spider,
I marked where on a little promontory it stood isolated,
Marked how to explore the vacant vast surrounding,
It launched forth filament, filament, filament, out of itself,
Ever unreeling them ever tirelessly speeding them.

And you, O my soul where you stand,
Surrounded, detached, in measureless oceans of space,
Ceaselessly musing, venturing, throwing, seeking the spheres to
                                            connect them,
Till the bridge you will need be formed, till the ductile anchor hold,
Till the gossamer thread you fling catch somewhere, O my soul.

Walt Whitman

235.   IN THIS STRANGE HOUSE

In this strange house of flesh confined
Heart must play host to tenant mind.

Occupants caught together here,
Both bolt their doors against one fear,

That monstrous menace all about
Which lurks within more than without.

While in this dwelling two abide
One feels, one thinks, him safe inside.

But if with pain mind is oppressed
Host can do nothing for his guest.

If a grave illness strike the host
Guest can do nothing. He is lost.

When this house burns the heart will die,
But mind from its fire, a phoenix, fly.

Carleton Drewry

236.   ONLY A BEAUTY, ONLY A POWER

. . . But in the darkest hour of night
When even the foxes peer for sight
The byre-cock crows; he feels the light.

So, in this water mixed with dust,
The byre-cock spirit crows from trust
That death will change because it must,

For all things change, the darkness changes,
The wandering spirits change their ranges,
The corn is gathered to the granges.

The corn is sown again, it grows,
The stars burn out, the darkness goes.
The rhythms change, they do not close.

They change, and we, who pass like foam,
Like dust blown through the streets of Rome,
Change ever, too; we have no home,

Only a beauty, only a power,
Sad in the fruit, bright in the flower,
Endlessly erring for its hour

But gathering, as we stray, a sense
Of Life, so lovely and intense,
It lingers when we wander hence.

That those who follow feel behind
Their backs, when all before is blind,
Our joy, a rampart to the mind.

John Masefield

237.   UNITY

One thing in all things have I seen:
One thought has haunted earth and air;
Clangour and silence both have been
In palace chambers. Everywhere

I saw the mystic vision flow
And live in men and woods and streams,
Until I could no longer know
The dream of life from my own dreams.

Sometimes it rose like fire in me
Within the depths of my own mind,
And spreading to infinity,
It took the voices of the wind:

It scrawled the human mystery—
Dim heraldry—on light and air;
Wavering along the starry sea
I saw the flying vision there.

Each fire that in God's temple lit
Burns fierce before the inner shrine,
Dimmed as my fire grew near to it
And darkened at the light of mine.

At last, at last, the meaning caught—
The spirit wears its diadem;
It shakes its wondrous plumes of thought
And trails the stars along with them.
                    AE (George William Russell)

238.   I COULD GIVE ALL TO TIME

To Time it never seems that he is brave
To set himself against the peaks of snow

To lay them level with the running wave,
Nor is he overjoyed when they lie low,
But only grave, contemplative and grave.

What now is inland shall be ocean isle,
Then eddies playing round a sunken reef
Like the curl at the corner of a smile;
And I could share Time's lack of joy or grief
At such a planetary change of style.

I could give all to Time—except
What I myself have held. But why declare
The things forbidden that while the Customs slept
I have crossed to Safety with? For I am There,
And what I would not part with I have kept.

Robert Frost

239.   LET THIS BE MY PARTING WORD

When I go from hence let this be my parting word, that what I
have seen is unsurpassable.

I have tasted of the hidden honey of this lotus that expands on the
ocean of light, and thus am I blessed—let this be my parting word.

In this playhouse of infinite forms I have had my play and here I
have caught sight of him that is formless.

My whole body and my limbs have thrilled with his touch who
is beyond touch; and if the end comes here, let it come—let this be
my parting word.

Rabindranath Tagore

240.   THE RECAPITULATION

Not through the rational mind,
But by elation coming to me
Sometimes, I am sure
Death is but a door.

A state of purity, sweet grace
It is, nor can last long,
But in that essence, I feel
Life beyond death is real.

Perhaps it is only the human need.
When reason rules, reason denies it.
But comes elation unto me
And blows God all through me.

When the flesh was young and strong
And the mind also, I denied God.
But time's sullen call
Has made my body fall.

Spirit of holy love, arise,
Meek and gentle, sweet and calm,
Arise in the ruthless world
And your truth put on.

To the rational mind grant
Things rational. But to the spirit
(All things there possible)
Accord what is spiritual.

Richard Eberhart

241.   HOLDERLIN

Now as before do you not hear their voices
Serene in the midst of their rejoicing
Chanting to those who have hopes and make choices
Clear as the birds in the thick summer foliage:
    It is! It is!
    We are! We are!

Clearly, as if they were us, and not us,
Hidden like the future, distant as the stars,

Having no more meaning than the fullness of music,
Chanting from the pure peaks where success,
Effort and desire are meaningless,
Surpassed at last in the joy of joy,
Chanting at last the blue's last view:
> It is! It is!
> This is eternity! Eternity is now!

Delmore Schwartz

242. AS KINGFISHERS CATCH FIRE

As kingfishers catch fire, dragonflies draw flame;
As tumbled over rim in roundy wells
Stones ring; like each tucked string tells, each hung bell's
Bow swung finds tongue to fling out broad its name;
Each mortal thing does one thing and the same:
Deals out that being indoors each one dwells;
Selves—goes itself; *myself* it speaks and spells,
Crying *What I do is me: for that I came.*

I say more: the just man justices;
Keeps grace: that keeps all his goings graces;
Acts in God's eye what in God's eye he is—
Christ—for Christ plays in ten thousand places,
Lovely in limbs, and lovely in eyes not his
To the Father through the features of men's faces.

Gerard Manley Hopkins

243. ALL THAT WAS MORTAL

All that was mortal shall be burned away,
  All that was mind shall have been put to sleep.
Only the spirit shall awake to say
  What the deep says to the deep;
But for an instant, for it too is fleeting—

As on a field with new snow everywhere,
Footprints of birds record a brief alighting
In flight begun and ended in the air.

Sara Teasdale

244.   IN AFTER TIME

In after time, when all this dream
Becomes pure dream, and roughest years
Lie down among the tender grass,
And spring up sentient upon the meadow;

In that after time of great-born Aprils,
Beyond a century of tatters and of malice,
When love has thrown out fear and madness
The eyes will see the sun as wonder.

In after time, when rage and chaos
Lose their sovereign force, new dream
Will lift the shining life to spirit
And mate the make of man to merit.

Then shall holy summers come; then laughter
God-like shake upon a dewy morning;
Then fullness grow, big with purpose,
And man shall know again his richness.

Richard Eberhart

245.   MAN IS GOD'S NATURE

The god would come, the god would go.
   The wind is never seen, but it is known
   In pelt of rain, in lace of snow.
So through our sense is godhead blown.

The least elusive, master imprint
    Taken in the impression of our faces
    Is a look not spirit's hint,
And more than intellectual graces.

The character that makes the form
    Is spiritual fact, that stands upon the flesh
    Becoming at last the human norm:
There the god is ever fresh.

We do not see the god, but give it
    In the subtlety of happy lineaments,
    When all our passions have been lit;
Godhead in the mortal element.

                                    Richard Eberhart

246.   NIGHT ON THE PRAIRIES

Night on the prairies;
The supper is over—the fire on the ground burns low;
The wearied emigrants sleep, wrapt in their blankets:
I walk by myself—I stand and look at the stars, which I think now I
                                    never realized before.

Now I absorb immortality and peace,
I admire death, and test propositions.

How plenteous! How spiritual!

I was thinking the day most splendid, till I saw what the not-day
                                    exhibited,
I was thinking this globe enough, till there sprang out so noiseless
                                    around me myriads of other globes.
Now, while the great thoughts of space and eternity fill me, I will
                                    measure myself by them;
And now, touch'd with the lives of other globes, arrived as far along
                                    as those of the earth,

Or waiting to arrive, or pass'd on farther than those of the earth,
I henceforth no more ignore them, than I ignore my own life,
Or the lives of the earth arrived as far as mine, or waiting to arrive.

O I see now that life cannot exhibit all to me—as the day cannot,
I see that I am to wait for what will be exhibited by death.

Walt Whitman

247.   THE IMMORTAL SPIRIT

The Immortal Spirit is that single ghost
Of every time incarnate in one time
Which to achieve its timelessness must climb
Our bodies, and in our senses be engrossed.
Without that Spirit within, our lives are lost
Fragments, disturbing the earth's rim.
Unless we will it live, that God pines, dim,
Ghost in our lives: its life, our death, the cost.

The Spirit of present, past, futurity
Seeks through the many-headed wills
To build the invisible visible city.
Shut in himself, each blind, beaked subject kills
His neighbor and himself, and shuts out pity
For that flame-winged Creator who fulfils.

Stephen Spender

248.   DIVINE POEMS: 74

Within the city of my death
Comes Death melancholy,
For that he seeks to reap me
Who gave God His Head.

Yet if he touch me, ah! he
Slays but the body alone,

Still upon its Throne
Shall sit my Head.

Poor Death! who can no
More call me dead
Unless he kill my Head:
And that forever is upon

His Shoulders and He proud
To wear it, His diadem
From Life, the gem
He died for. So Death—*I live!*
                    José Garcia Villa

249.   SAILING TO BYZANTIUM

I

That is no country for old men. The young
In one another's arms, birds in the trees
—Those dying generations—at their song,
The salmon-falls, the mackerel-crowded seas,
Fish, flesh, or fowl, commend all summer long
Whatever is begotten, born, and dies.
Caught in that sensual music all neglect
Monuments of unageing intellect.

II

An aged man is but a paltry thing,
A tattered coat upon a stick, unless
Soul clap its hands and sing, and louder sing
For every tatter in its mortal dress,
Nor is there singing school but studying
Monuments of its own magnificence;
And therefore I have sailed the seas and come
To the holy city of Byzantium.

III

O sages standing in God's holy fire
As in the gold mosaic of a wall,
Come from the holy fire, pern in a gyre
And be the singing-masters of my soul.
Consume my heart away; sick with desire
And fastened to a dying animal
It knows not what it is; and gather me
Into the artifice of eternity.

IV

Once out of nature I shall never take
My bodily form from any natural thing,
But such a form as Grecian goldsmiths make
Of hammered gold and gold enamelling
To keep a drowsy Emperor awake;
Or set upon a golden bough to sing
To lords and ladies of Byzantium
Of what is past, or passing, or to come.

William Butler Yeats

250.   AND DEATH SHALL HAVE NO DOMINION

And death shall have no dominion.
Dead men naked they shall be one
With the man in the wind and the west moon;
When their bones are picked clean and the clean bones gone,
They shall have stars at elbow and foot;
Though they go mad they shall be sane,
Though they sink through the sea they shall rise again;
Though lovers be lost love shall not;
And death shall have no dominion.

And death shall have no dominion.
Under the windings of the sea
They lying long shall not die windily;
Twisting on racks when sinews give way,
Strapped to a wheel, yet they shall not break;
Faith in their hands shall snap in two,
And the unicorn evils run them through;
Split all ends up they shan't crack;
And death shall have no dominion.

And death shall have no dominion.
No more may gulls cry at their ears
Or waves break loud on the seashores;
Where blew a flower may a flower no more
Lift its head to the blows of the rain;
Though they be mad and dead as nails,
Heads of the characters hammer through daisies;
Break in the sun till the sun breaks down,
And death shall have no dominion.

Dylan Thomas

251.   PASSAGE TO MORE THAN INDIA

From "Passage to India"

O Thou transcendent!
Nameless—the fibre and the breath!
Light of the light—shedding forth universes—the centre of them!
Thou mightier centre of the true, the good, the loving!
Thou moral, spiritual fountain! affection's source! thou reservoir!
Thou pulse! thou motive of the stars, suns, systems,
That, circling, move in order, safe, harmonious,
Athwart the shapeless vastnesses of space!
How should I think—how breathe a single breath—how speak—if, out
                                                        of myself,
I could not launch, to those, superior universes?

Passage to more than India!
Are thy wings plumed indeed for such far flights?
O Soul, voyagest thou indeed on voyages like these?
Disportest thou on waters such as these?
Soundest below the Sanscrit and the Vedas?
Then have thy bent unleashed.

Passage to you, your shores, ye aged fierce enigmas!
Passage to you, to mastership of you, ye strangling problems!
You, strewed with the wrecks of skeletons, that, living, never reached
                                                                    you.

Passage—immediate passage! the blood burns in my veins!
Away, O soul! hoist instantly the anchor!
Cut the hawsers—haul out—shake out every sail!
Have we not stood here like trees in the ground long enough?
Have we not grovelled here long enough, eating and drinking like
                                                            mere brutes?
Have we not darkened and dazed ourselves with books long enough?

Sail forth! steer for the deep waters only!
Reckless, O soul, exploring, I with thee, and thou with me;
For we are bound where mariner has not yet dared to go,
And we will risk the ship, ourselves and all.

O my brave soul!
O farther, farther sail!
O daring joy, but safe! Are they not all the seas of God?
O farther, farther, farther sail.

                                                        Walt Whitman

index of authors

References are to poem numbers

index of first lines

References are to poem numbers

DATE DUE